THE MAGICIAN'S KABBALAH

KABBALAH AS AN INITIATORY PATH ILLUSTRATED BY TAROT

Marcus Katz

First Edition published by Forge Press, Keswick, 2015.

ISBN-13: 978-0955856617

Dedication

Dedicated to those who labour in the orchard.

To Soror C. L. and Frater V. S. L. of the O. E. D.

And As Ever, Above All, this work is dedicated to

Antistita Astri Argentei

The Priestess of the Silver Star

She whose light leads the way to the *Arcanum Arcanorum*, the Secret of Secrets

Vos Vos Vos Vos

V.V.V.V.

About the Author

Marcus Katz has been working with and teaching Western Esotericism, Kabbalah and tarot for over twenty-five years. He also works with apprentices in the Western Esoteric Initiatory System® and was the first student to gain a Masters Degree in Western Esotericism from the University of Exeter, consolidating his practical study of the Kabbalah and Ritual.

He was first introduced to Kabbalah thirty years ago through the works of Dion Fortune and Aleister Crowley and has made a daily study and practice of the subject since that time. He worked through the syllabus of the International School of Kabbalah in the 1980's before going on to study traditional Kabbalah for twenty years, including attendance at conferences worldwide with presenters including Moshe Idel and other leading scholars of the subject.

He co-founded the Tarosophy Tarot Association, the world's largest professional tarot Association, with Tali Goodwin in 2009. His first book, *Tarosophy*, was called a "major contribution" to tarot by Rachel Pollack. He has written many other titles on the tarot, Alchemy, Kabbalah and related subjects, including his journal of the Abramelin Operation, a perilous and intense ritual to gain the knowledge and conversation of the Holy Guardian Angel, which has been published as *After the Angel*.

His ongoing *magnum opus* on the Western Esoteric Initiatory System (WEIS), published as the MAGISTER (in 11 volumes) has been described as "audacious" and "staggering".

He lives in the Lake District with his wife, fellow author and editor, Brina, and magician's cat, Alex, whose full name is Alexander Calvert Esq. M.M. (Master Mouser).

Marcus offers a unique apprenticeship opportunity to engage with the Great Work of spiritual liberation through the Western Esoteric Initiatory System, which can be discovered at:

www.westernesotericism.com

The many benefits of joining the Tarosophy Tarot Association are available at:

www.tarotassociation.net.

Acknowledgements

I would like to acknowledge those students who have worked through early iterations of this material through the Crucible Club, Order of Everlasting Day and Magicka School.

I would also like to acknowledge the scholars and professors who refined my work whilst I studied at the University of Exeter.

The librarians and archive custodians of the British Museum, British Library, Library & Museum of Freemasonry, Ritman Library (Amsterdam), and Warburg Institute have all given of their time and service in the provision of material which has informed this present work.

Contents

Introduction: A Guide for the Perplexed 10

   A Note on Spelling 15

   Using This Book...16

The Tarot, Ancient Egypt & Kabbalah 18

The Tarot in the Golden Dawn...29

   The Tarot and Tree of Life...35

   The Sephiroth...42

   The Golden Dawn System 46

      The Grades of the Golden Dawn...52

      The Tree of the Golden Dawn...54

   The Tree of Night Before the Dawn 68

   Aleister Crowley's Variation to the GD System...70

   The Waite-Trinick System 73

The Tree of Sapphires 90

   Voices of the Word, Leaves of the Light 90

   The Tree as a Meta-model (Template Theory) 96

   The Tree as a Fractal System (The Orchard) 101

   The Tree as an Emanative System (The Fountain of Light) 102

   The Tree as a Communications System (Lattice Theory) 104

The Sephiroth and the Four Worlds...111

   The Four Worlds 114

Ain Soph Aur: A Necessary Non-Negation 122

   Aleph in Kether 123

   Yod in Chockmah 124

   Nun in Binah...125

Kether: The Crown of Coherent Light 128

The Doctrine of Trans-Resonance 128

The Triune Crown 130

    Kaph in Kether 130

    Tau in Chockmah 131

    Resh in Binah 132

The Tree of Crowns 134

Chockmah: The Quarry of Devotion 137

Binah: The Angel of the Tides 145

Chesed: The Unicorn at the Waystation 152

Geburah: The Folding of the Robe 159

Tiphareth: The Hub of Sacrifice 169

The Paths Of the Heart 171

    A. The God of the Heart 171

    B. The Initiation of the Heart 171

    C. The Trials of the Heart 172

The Lines of Sacrifice 173

Netzach: The Rose in the Lamplight 177

Hod: The Crystal Watercourse 182

Yesod: The Hall of Mirrors 187

Malkuth: The Kingdom of the Shells 193

The Klippoth: The Shells & Husks 201

Gematria: The Numerology of the Kabbalah 209

The Binary System 211

The Grade Passwords 212

The Twenty-Two Paths 216

The Psyche: A Curtain of Souls 228

The Soul in Ancient Egypt 231

Contemporary Kabbalah 234

The Scholarly 234

The New Age 235

The Occult 235

The Popular & Literary 236

Conclusion 237

Appendix: A Kabbalah Study Program 239

Bibliography 242

Kindle Tarot Books & Series 251

Introduction: A Guide for the Perplexed

> It was by the knowledge of the attribution of the Paths and the Tarot keys that Daniel deciphered the meaning of the MENE, MENE, TEKEL UPHARSIN.
>
> - Previously unpublished note from the original Golden Dawn mss., likely attrib. S. L. MacGregor Mathers.

In this book we will take a tour of both tarot and Kabbalah, specifically the diagram known as the Tree of Life. It should be first said – very clearly – that there is no ancient historical connection of Kabbalah and tarot. However, as both provide maps of our experience arising from profound examination of that same experience, they find deep correspondences which are useful to all spiritual journeyers.

These two subjects are both extremely wide and diverse and we list many other titles in the bibliography for your further study. Kabbalah in particular is complex, no matter how we look at it, so we have endeavoured to make it accessible whilst pointing to interesting avenues of exploration. In this present book we are specifically looking at the illustration of the Western Esoteric Initiatory System (WEIS) by tarot on the Tree of Life. The WEIS is an authentic system of spiritual development attuned to a western contemporary life.[1]

---

[1] See Katz, M. *The Magister Vol. 0.*

Kabbalah, illustrated by tarot, despite (in fact, because of) its complexity, provides us an incredibly flexible tool of comprehension with numerous functions, including but not limited to:

Scientific – as a working **model** of any act of nature and creation, from the personal to the universal.

Religious – as an **account** of the nature of the divine, our spiritual role and the relationship of our life to the divine.

Art – as an **illustration** of our experience of nature.

Mysticism – as a **structure** to comprehend and predict profound and personal transcendent experience.

Magical – as a **tool** for engaging with the universe in diverse ways to accomplish our intent.

Psychological – as a **map** of human behaviour.

Initiatory – as a **system** by which an individual might arise to the realisation of the divine and their true nature.

I also hope to provide many other aspects of correspondence between the two systems that will provide practical enhancement of your tarot reading, and new ways of accessing Kabbalah to those already familiar with tarot. To those versed in Kabbalah, I trust this book will remain true to most of the major streams of the tradition, whilst demonstrating how tarot illustrates the Tree of Life to further illuminate these ideas in a new way.

If you are an absolute beginner to either subject, I recommend *Tarosophy* by myself and *Around the Tarot in 78 Days* with co-author Tali Goodwin as foundation tarot books to this present work. If you are new to Kabbalah, particularly in relation to tarot, we have written a foundation book *Kabbalah and Tarot* under our pen-name, Andrea Green, which contains more immediate and practical tarot applications of Kabbalah.

Let us first consider the history of our subjects. The tarot as we know it arose in the 15th Century in Italy – around the same time as the Gutenberg Bible became the first book to be printed in movable type. We presently have no record of anything other than dissimilar card games prior to that time. Whilst there are many methods of divination dating back to antiquity, the use of tarot for divination was comparatively recent. It began as a card game, became a family heirloom of choice, and only then finally became associated with fortune-telling and in parallel, western esotericism.

There is also no historical connection between the tarot and gypsies of any description for much the same reason – there is no ancient history of tarot. The records of the various peoples known as gypsies providing fortune-telling are illustrated with playing cards, not tarot. It was really not until the 1950's that a fictional connection between gypsies, pyramids, owls, skulls and the tarot cards from 1910 (Waite-Smith) became popularized by marketing and advertising which then became fixed into a common contemporary misunderstanding.[2]

As we will come to see, the first connection of tarot and Kabbalah came through a piece of writing in Antoine Court de Gébelin's *Le Monde Primitif*, which was published in 1781. A contributing author to these volumes of analysis of the ancient world, the Comte de Mellett, about who comparatively little is known, wrote that there was a connection between the 22 Major cards of the tarot to the 22 Hebrew letters.[3] It is this idea, published only a little over two hundred years ago, that gave rise to the connection between Kabbalah – the Jewish system of mysticism – and tarot cards.

---

[2] See Katz, M., 'Tarot on the Threshold: Liminality and Illegitimate Knowledge' in Auger, E. (ed) *Tarot in Culture, Vol I*. p. 274-7.

[3] The identity of Comte de Mellet is now known to be Louis-Raphaël-Lucrèce de Fayolle, according to the work of historian Robin Briggs. See Dummett, M. *The Game of Tarot*, p. 105, fn. 13, repeated also in Huson, P. *Mystical Origins of the Tarot: From Ancient Roots to Modern Usage*, p. 54.

However, the correspondences between the two systems were uncertain and changeable, as the structure of the tarot – notably the ordering of the Major Arcana cards, was not agreed upon by these early authors, including Etteilla (1738 – 1791), who arguably became the world's first tarot teacher.[4]

Whilst authors such as Etteilla took the ideas in de Gébelin and produced new works on tarot cards for cartomancy (fortune-telling) other authors took a wider scope and connected the cards to not only ancient Egypt (as originally popularized in de Gébelin) but to Kabbalah. Again, this is only within the last two centuries, and no earlier.

In Europe, the rise of a wave of esotericism took these ideas and wove them into the expanding awareness of Kabbalah, to create a synthesis of thought that has been called by one leading scholar of traditional Kabbalah, a "supreme charlatanism".[5]

This "charlatanism" however, led to a productive wave of writing and consideration of the universe. It was French occultist Eliphas Levi (1810 – 1875) who can be seen first to use the Kabbalah as a universal map of esoteric thought, modelling not only the chapters of his books on the structure of the Hebrew letters – and hence Kabbalah and through correspondence, tarot – but also much of his writing. There are sections in his works of text and poetry that deliberately and explicitly follow the sequence of Hebrew letters and their correspondences to both tarot and Kabbalah.[6]

This usage inspired the founding members of the Golden Dawn in 1888, and in parallel, esotericists such as Aleister Crowley (1875 – 1947) and A. E. Waite (1857 – 1942), who both immersed themselves in the symbolic synthesis of tarot and Kabbalah as a map of the initiatory system, and designed it into their decks – and hence every deck that has modelled itself on their designs.

---

[4] Dummett, *ibid*, pp. 108-9.
[5] Scholem, G. *Kabbalah*, p. 203.
[6] Levi, E. *The Book of Splendours*, pp. 127-42.

So a creative misunderstanding is now hard-wired into many tarot decks whether their designers are aware of Kabbalah or otherwise. In further understanding Kabbalah, we can unlock many of the designs and symbolic intent of the first esoteric tarot decks, particularly with regard to the Initiatory System and as a Universal Map of Creation.

In this present book we propose that the WEIS has been constructed for at least four centuries as a synthesis of Neo-Platonic, Gnostic, Hermetic, and Rosicrucian philosophy, delivered through systems as diverse as astrology, tarot, alchemy, and Kabbalah. We further present this work as providing an authentic and valid practice of mundane, magical, mystical and spiritual appreciation. We believe it is also of contemporary relevance and accessibility through its illustration by the widely recognized tarot images.[7]

This is a book intended for intermediate students of tarot who are familiar with its language and have experience in reading it as a map of self-awareness and spiritual development. The reader may find themselves wondering of the relevance of various sections, numerological analysis, or apparently far-fetched links of correspondence. This is to be expected, as the process of Kabbalah is one which must be experienced, not merely studied; the mental exercise of forming links of correspondence, as one example, ultimately re-programs the brain to do something more – and something truly magical that cannot be communicated, only experienced.

As mentioned above, we have another title, *Kabbalah and Tarot: A Step-Up Guide*, under our pen-name Andrea Green, which is intended for absolute beginners and a companion work to this present book. It includes several practical and accessible exercises to tune up comprehension of Kabbalistic concepts. We also provide later a large list of recommended books with brief commentary to

---

[7] We teach the WEIS through the Crucible Club and Order of the Everlasting Day which can be discovered at www.westernesotericism.com.

guide your further work in Kabbalah, in addition to an online course for self-study which shares material to this book.

In this present book we will look at the history and concepts of Kabbalah, and its appropriation by Western Esotericism. We will specifically look at three maps of spiritual ascent – Golden Dawn, Waite-Trinick and Crowley – illustrated by the tarot. In doing so we will draw upon secret images that have been hidden for a century, only recently discovered and published in our books, *Abiding in the Sanctuary*, *A New Dawn for Tarot*, *The Tarot of the Secret Dawn*, *Secrets of the Waite-Smith Tarot* and *The Magister*. This present work is a key-stone of Kabbalah for these other titles.

I hope to demonstrate the reasonability and usefulness of using Kabbalah and tarot together, both for divination and contemplation, and with particular regard to the spiritual understanding of our condition – both present and potential.

A Note on Spelling
There are no vowel letters in Hebrew, so the word 'Kabbalah' is a transliteration of Hebrew letters, and can be spelt in English as sounded, variously, 'Kabbalah', 'Qabalah', 'Cabbalah', etc.

The general usage by Jewish scholars is 'Kabbalah', (i.e. Moshe Idel and Gershom Scholem) which is that which is adopted here. In general, although it is not a universal rule, the usage 'Qabalah' has often been adopted by occultists and New Age authors (i.e. Dion Fortune, Naomi Ozaniec, Gareth Knight and R. J. Stewart), and 'Cabbalah' by the earlier Christian authors on the subject.

I have italicized most Hebrew transliterated words other than those in common usage such as Kabbalah, to remind the reader these are English characters for a Hebrew word, originally spelt in Hebrew letters. I have not used Hebrew characters for clarity and to avoid formatting complications in e-book versions. I have generally kept "tarot" rather than "Tarot" for ease of reading.

Using This Book

Kabbalah is a complex and profound subject and any attempt to make it accessible is made difficult by the language alone – before even straying into complex Judaic philosophy and history. There will be sections of this present book that will on first reading appear to be written in code or have no relevance to daily experience. The meaning or relevance of a complex phrase such as that below may be impossible to read at first attempt:

> Numerically, *Malkuth* values 496, which totals to 19 (4+9+6), which totals to 10 (1+9), which can be broken down to 1 as well. Thus, *Malkuth* (10) and *Kether* (1) are within the value of *Malkuth* itself. *Kether*, on the other hand, values 620 (the *Zohar* speaks of the 620 pillars of light), which breaks down to 8 (6+2), the number of the *Sephirah Hod*...

It is recommended that readers persevere with the learning of correspondences, the names of the *Sephiroth*, the Hebrew letters, the positions and relationships of the *Sephiroth* on the Tree of Life and the tarot images. As you construct this basic framework, the more obscure elements will slowly fall into place as they become relevant to your experience. A general study guide has been provided as an appendix for those wishing a suggestion of an ordered sequence of learning.

For the contemporary reader who requires an alternative version of this book without reference to its original context, you may like to use the following substitution table throughout:

> All Numbers and Letters: The way in which we relate to the universe through language and pattern.

> Divine: The patterns that arise in the way in which we experience the universe.

> God: The universe.

> Kabbalah: A way of looking at the universe.

Sephiroth: Aspects of the universe.

Tarot: Illustrations of significant landmarks and signposts on the map.

Tree of Life: A map of one way of looking at the universe.

Whilst this is somewhat of a simplistic key, it may assist the casual reader to see the Kabbalah as a model with some relevance to their experience. All use of Gematria and Correspondence throughout the following book can be seen in this light as simply 'mental exercises to see the universe in lots of different ways' and safely ignored unless they serve this purpose.

We will now look further at the history and connections of tarot and Kabbalah, particularly with regard to the Hebrew letters.

The Tarot, Ancient Egypt & Kabbalah

We must first look to the work of Comte de Mellet in *Le Monde Primitif* to appreciate the earliest roots of the correspondence of tarot and Kabbalah. I have in the text below referenced the original volume of *Le Monde Primitif* which can be viewed at Gallica (Bibliothèque nationale de France), both the two existing English translations and a French typescript.[8]

The main proposal of the work was that the twenty-two Major Arcana of the tarot cards were letters, or tableaux, which together could be arranged to form sentences and language, as it was seen that the hieroglyphs were similar; pictures instead of letters. There was a mere footnote that "the Hebrew language has 22 letters" whilst the main text focused on the alleged Egyptian connection.

Already though, the twenty-two Arcana were seen as a progressive narrative, in this early instance as a grand story of the Ages – a theme that would later be reflected in the work of both Levi and Crowley.[9]

In brief, the Major Arcana were seen as telling the story of the three Ages of Gold, Silver and Bronze (or Iron), in three series of seven cards, as follows:

> **Gold**: The Universe (World) gives birth to mankind (Judgement) and then are created the Sun (Sun), Moon (Moon), Stars and fish (Star, corresponding to Aquarius). There is a fall from heaven (Tower) and the Devil (Devil) comes to end the Golden Age.

> **Silver**: We are led by an Angel (Temperance) who teaches us to live and try and avoid death (Death) and accident (Hanged Man) now we are no longer in the Golden Age. We are assisted in this by our strength to cultivate ourselves and

---

[8] See http://gallica.bnf.fr/ [search for Gebelin], the work of Donald Tyson [no longer available online at the original source but available in PDF format at various locations] and Karlin, J. *Rhapsodies of the Bizarre*.
[9] Katz. M. *The Magister*, pp. 89-98.

resist our own wildness (Strength). In coming to realise we now live in an inconstant and changing world (Wheel) we seek (Hermit) Justice (Justice).

Bronze/Iron: In the wars that follow (Chariot) we are caught between vice and virtue, no longer led by reason (Lovers). We raise religions and rules (Hierophant) and set Kings (Emperor) and Queens (Empress) upon the earth. This leads the people to pride, idolatry [High Priestess as Junon and the Peacock] and deception (Magician).

This leads to the eventual madness of our race, which is seen as the Fool card, where the tiger biting his legs is viewed as "remorse" trying to delay our inevitable march towards folly and crimes.

The four Suits were seen as representing four forms of divination, as to prove the utilisation of tarot for fortune-telling and divinatory means:

Wands: The wands of magicians, the casting of lots.

Cups: Divination by cups, bowls and reflections.

Swords: The divination of the future by the fall of a sword, arrows or axe.

Pentacles: The use of talismans and engravings.

The essay provides us only a few explicit correspondences of the Hebrew letters to the tarot, but enough to see that the 22 letters were assigned in order to the sequence of tarot starting with the World and ending with the Magician, with the Fool card as the final letter Tau. This sequence follows the same ordering as in the story given by Comte de Mellet.

Aleph: World

Beth: Judgement

Gimel: Sun

Daleth:	Moon
Heh:	Star
Vau:	Tower
Zayin:	Devil (Typhon)
Cheth:	Temperance
Teth:	Death
Yod:	Hermit (Prudence)
Kaph:	Strength
Lamed:	Wheel of Fortune
Mem:	Hermit
Nun:	Justice
Samekh:	Chariot
Ayin:	Lovers
Peh:	Hierophant
Tzaddi:	Emperor
Qoph:	Empress
Resh:	High Priestess
Shin:	Magician
Tau:	Fool

We have presently no evidence that these correspondences were in circulation prior to Comte de Mellet presenting them in Court de Gébelin's work although it is difficult to concede they were created *ex nihilo* without some prior consideration. If they were developed in Freemasonic circles prior to this publication, they were kept secret and have not yet been recovered. Whatever their genesis, the correspondence of the two systems would not have been much earlier than this publication in 1781.

There are a few examples in the text to suggest some consideration of the correspondences, for example, the un-numbered Fool is seen as not signifying anything other than itself, and so is a *Tau* or 'sign' in its simplicity. This is a literal meaning of the Hebrew letter, which have values and meanings – and also spellings, beyond being simply a letter. The letter *Lamed*, for example, means also 'ox-goad' and is seen by Comte de Mellet as representing the severe rule of fate corresponding to the Wheel of Fortune. However, the letter *Teth* corresponding to Death is seen as a symbol for 'reaping', whereas the letter means 'snake'. It appears as if the correspondences have been constructed by their simple ordering to the sequence of tarot as given by the authors, and then explained on the shape of the letters themselves, rather than on their positions on the Tree of Life, their literal meaning, or any other more complex reasoning.

We should also note that hidden inside this sequence of correspondences is something rather interesting that would not surface again for another century or so; when in 1904, Aleister Crowley 'received' his *Book of the Law* in which was written "*Tzaddi* is not the Star". When Crowley re-worked the correspondences and made the switch of *Tzaddi* and *Heh* to correspond with the Emperor and the Star, he returned those two letters to their respective positions given in the original 1781 system by Comte de Mellet.

Here are the Hebrew letters, values and their most common meanings.

Value	Letter Name	Letter	Pictograph	Letter in full	Value in full	Translations
1	Aleph	A	An Ox	ALPh	111	Ox, to create thousands, domesticate, one, thousand, clan, cattle, to learn, train, tame, teach, community, family
2	Beth	B	A House	BYTh	412	House, temple, daughter, tribe, tent, stanza, palace, dwelling place, receptacle, interior, place where things are found

3	Gimel	G	A Camel	GML (GYML)	73 (83)	Camel, camel driver, maturity, to wean, ripen, deal with, to do, perform, accomplish, to requite
4	Daleth	D	A Door	DLTh	434	Folding door, portal, gate, opening, page(scroll), first half of verse
5	Heh	H	A Man with raised arms	HA	6	Air hole, lattice window, existence, to be, Lo!, behold, this, the
6	Vau	V/W	A Hook	VV	12	Nail, pin, hook, fastening, peg
7	Zain	Z	A Weapon	ZYN	717	Sword, armour, spear, weapon, to equip, arm

8	Cheth	Ch	A Twisted hank	ChYTh	418	Fence, barrier, enclosure, awe, fear, cord
9	Teth	T	A Sign	TYTh	419	Snake, coiling, twisting, winding, leather bottle, sketch, draft, clay
10	Yod	T/Y/J	A Hand	YVD	20	Hand, clenched fist, power, strength, assistance, axle, tenon, side
20,500	Kaph	K	The Palm of a Hand	KPh	820	Palm of hand, bent hand, fist, weigh in hand, sole of foot, spoon, pan, dish, handle, twig, branch, hollow cave, cave, vault

30	Lamed	L	Spur or Goad	LMD	74	Ox Goad, learn by rote, study, practice, teach, train, instruct, studied, deduced, defined
40,600	Mem	M	Water	MYM	650	Water
50,700	Nun	N	A Serpent	NVN	756	Fish, flower, decay, waste away, deteriorate, to sprout, spread, flourish
60	Samekh	S	A Fish	SMKh	600	Prop, support, lean, assist
70	Ayin	A'a	An Eye	AYN	711	Eye, eye of mind, to study, source, spring, fountain, ring, hole, sight, face, look, appearance, surface, sparkling or bead of wine

80,800	Peh	P/Ph	A Mouth	PA, PY or PH	81, 90 or 85	Mouth
90,900	Tzaddi	Tz	An Arrow	TzDY	104	Fish hook, righteousness
100	Qoph	Q	A Needle-eye	QVPh	906	Back of head, ear, monkey, ape, eye of needle, bow
200	Resh	R	A Head	RYSh	510	Head, poverty
300	Shin	Sh	A Tooth	ShYN	1010	Tooth, molar
400	Tau	T	A Sign	TV	15	Cross, mark, sign, musical note

When using this table, you can refer to any Hebrew word and find its letters, so that a word spelt (and pronounced) as 'Kabbalah' is the English from the transliterated letters QBLH, *Qoph* + *Beth* + *Lamed* + *Heh* (which means 'receiving' or 'tradition'). Whilst Hebrew is written and read from right to left, we transliterate and represent the letters left to right in English, so we would not write HLBQ when showing the transliteration of Kabbalah.

In Gematria, the system of numerology we will look at later in this book, some letters have a different value if they appear within a word or at the end of the word, such as *Tzaddi*. If that letter is at the end of a word it has the value 900. The characters of these letters are also represented differently in their Hebrew character.

Here are the Hebrew characters themselves. We have avoided using them in this book for clarity, although it is essential for any deeper study of Kabbalah that you are familiar with the characters and can write them – in traditional Kabbalah this would be a ground-rule, although of course traditional Kabbalists would already be fluent in Hebrew.

א	ב	ג	ד	ה
Aleph	Beth	Gimel	Daleth	Heh

ו	ז	ח	ט	י
Vau	Zain	Cheth	Teth	Yod

דכ	ל	מ	נן	ס
Kaph	Lamed	Mem	Nun	Samekh

ע	פף	יצ	ק	ר
Ayin	Peh	Tzaddi	Qoph	Resh

ש	ת
Shin	Tau

Having surveyed this historic origin of the connection between Kabbalah and tarot (and introduced the Hebrew letters) we will now turn to the Golden Dawn who then went on to create a staggering synthesis of systems which incorporated this correspondence. In doing so they further consolidated the connection of tarot and Kabbalah in popular awareness.

The Tarot in the Golden Dawn

The Golden Dawn placed particular emphasis on the 22 Major Arcana cards of the tarot. They also had a specific symbolism in the cards which was used to illustrate the initiatory journey up the Tree of Life. The cards were shown to initiates, often for the first time, during elaborate rituals and presented with accompanying teaching as to their significance.

In the previously unpublished original papers of the Hermetic Order of the Golden Dawn, founded in 1888, is a series of typescript documents which list tarot descriptions and conclude with a note by one of its three founders, S. L. Macgregor Mathers. It is possible these descriptions are the foundation of Waite's knowledge of tarot both for the Waite-Smith Tarot and the Waite-Trinick Tarot.

Whilst we cover the specific details of the Golden Dawn original material in *A New Dawn for Tarot* (Forge Press, 2014) with illustrations of the cards from the archives and *Tarot of the Secret Dawn* (a 22-Major Arcana deck based on the scrying of a Golden Dawn adept, with accompanying booklet) we produce here the first publication of these Golden Dawn descriptions.[10]

TAROT TRUMPS

"Spirit of Ether"

0 [Aleph] FOOL: Man like the Greek Mercury — bounding up from the earth — the animal from behind him dragging him down. Caduceus of [missing symbol, probably Mercury] over his shoulder - represents spiritual power restrained by material conditions.

(Animal has him by the Heel)

"Magus of Power"

---

[10] Our thanks to Tony Fuller for reminding us about this piece of the mss. which we omitted from *A New Dawn for Tarot*.

1 [Beth] MAGICIAN: Magician with Altar and Z-A-M [Zelator Adeptus Minor] lesser implements before him – invoking.

2 [Gimel] HIGH PRIESTESS: Priestess – between two G.D. Pillars like Hegemone (Red Black Lamen and Collar)

"Priestess of the Silver Star"

3 [Daleth] EMPRESS: Seated – Winged Empress with Dove – (7 Pointed Crown and Heptagram on Sceptre)

"Daughter of the Mighty Ones"

4 [Heh] EMPEROR Crowned Warrior – Lightening on Shield. Thunder Cloud beneath feet.

"Son of the Morning Chief among the Mighty"

5 [Vau] HIEROPHANT: Osiris between two columns 2 or 4 Kneeling figures and an altar before him. (Bull, Apis, Sign of OSIRIS) (Nevis of RA) A Triple barred [symbol missing] like that on which Nehushtan is twined. 4 figures (4 Letters of Name – King, Queen, Prince, Princess, Osiris – in middle above).

"Magus of the Eternal Gods"

6 [Zain] THE LOVERS: Angel sends down radiant light upon two figures which balance on either side - the two figures partly light partly dark varying – mediumship of a central figure – oracle of the mighty Gods (the Good and Evil woman, man between)

"Children of the Voice Divine, the Oracles of the Mighty Gods"

7 [Cheth] CHARIOT: Sea horses of Neptune – Triumphal figure (not Neptune) (Solar figure).

"Child of the Powers of the Waters Lord of the Triumph of Life"

8 [Teth] STRENGTH: Winged head dress – queenly figure seated - Hand resting on a lion – coercing it. (Holding lion by Chain Collar Lion dragging away)

"Daughter of the Flaming Sword Leader of the Lion"

9 [Yod] HERMIT: White head - light streaming on to it like a tonsure. Holds Globular Lantern. (Sphere of Tiphareth)

"Magus of the Voice of Light, the Prophet of the Gods"

10 [Lamed] JUSTICE: Like the Card in use "Justice".[11]

"Daughter of the Lords of truth, the holder of the Balance"

11 [Kaph] WHEEL OF FORTUNE

[Pencil sketch of Wheel with spokes, and signs of zodiac and Ashtaroth written below]

Wheel of 12 - Spokes - 4 Sphinxes made of Signs of Zodiac.

At Top – Woman-headed, Lion-bodied Sphinx holding Scales.

Descending - Goat headed centaur with Scorpion tail (or a Scorpion man or horse as has been found on Assyrian boundary stones)

At foot - Virgin's head with fish's body - Clothed in leopard skin (woman to the waist)

Ascending - Human headed bull of Assyria tail like a bird

Behind the Wheel a shadowy Angel figure affirming the Higher – Ashtaroth written below on the lowest part of the wheel.

"Lord of the Forces of Life"

12 [Mem] HANGED MAN: A drowned giant in the shape of [pencil sketch of figure lying on side with legs in swastica position] Swastica

---

[11] We believe this refers to a Marseilles or other European deck as found in Westcott's private collection, for example, see Bain, D. *A New Dawn for Tarot*.

Cross - Between the rocky bed of the ocean and the bottom of Ark - full face, legs crossed, - rainbow at feet (Should be held sideways)

[Sketch of figure on side with rudimentary rainbow at feet].

"Spirit of the Mighty Waters"

13 [Nun] DEATH: Skeleton reaping fresh Vegetation coming from corrupted bodies. Extremities are 4 elements and [symbol of circle with eight spokes for spirit] two Heads - is crowned [symbol of Tau cross although 'cross of life' would refer to Ankh] form top of scythe - Cross of Life. Seed behind skeleton - unborn – nameless one.

In front Scorpion - ruthless destruction Snake - deception. Good and Evil. Eagle - Divine nature receiving life (Harmony from Chaos).

"Child of the Great Transformers Lord of the Gates of Death"

14 [Samekh] TEMPERANCE: Angel. 5 Star crown and Halo of Light - Wings Pours together fiery water and watery fire.

"Daughter of the Reconcilers, the Bringers forth of Life"

15 [Ayin] DEVIL: Goat headed demon stands on Cube left hand down Torch [symbols of Sun & Capricorn] Circle in centre of Cube 2 small demons male under Torch Female under Horn of Water hold cords attached to Circle in their hands. bat wings – hairy body. Sexual. Pentagram of light over head two Pents. Under feet invern pent on Face.

"Lord of the Gates of Matter, Child of the forces of time."

16 [Samekh] TOWER: the Power of the tread [likely 'triad'] destroying the columns of darkness. establishes itself in the 3 holes rent in the wall. The Kings of Edom fall out as crowned men. Right hand – Light. Left hand - Darkness.

"Lord of the Hosts of the Mighty"

17 [Tzaddi] THE STAR: Star has 7 and 14 Rays - Heptad multiplied by Triad – 21 – Eheich Sirius - Star of ISIS – SOTHIS

Woman - Synthesis of ISIS Neptune Athor Amiah and Binah

Great Supernal Mother pouring on Earth Waters of Creation which unite and form a river at her feet influence of Chokmah – binah and restored world.

Bird of Hermes on Tree of Knowledge.

Tree of Life on opposite side.

[Symbol of Mars] over woman's head.

Heptagram on her head

[Symbol of Venus] over bird of Hermes

[Symbol of Aquarius] Firmament dividing & Containing the Waters

[Symbols of Jupiter, Sun & Venus in a column to left, with Saturn, Moon and Mercury to right in column, and Mars in centre]

"Daughter of the Firmament, the Dweller between the Waters"

18 [Qoph] MOON: Moon on Side of increase. 4 [Yods] falling 32 rays – path of yetzirah. Jackals of Aunbri's [Anubis] guarding Gates of East and West, one standing one lying down [pencil sketch of figures] Crayfish or Scarabeus. Two Towers. Stream from horizon.

"Ruler of Flux and Reflux, the Child of the Sons of the Mighty"

19 [Resh] SUN: 12 Rays waved & salient alternately.

36 Secondary Rays

72 Tertiary Rays

7 [missing symbol, likely Yods] on each side falling

Portions of Circular wall

Children on water and earth. [sketch of two figures].

"Lord of the Fire of the World"

20. [Shin] JUDGMENT: Angel crowned with Sun. Surrounded by Rainbow in which leap Seraphim. Trumpet - influence of Spirit descending from Binah banner Ert [Sketch of Banner with Cross]

Pluto emerging from Volcanic rock. ISIS Full face NEPTHYS profile coming from Water. HORUS rises from Cubic Tomb in [Sketch of arms in 2=9 sign]

Centre 7 [Yods] descend in rays of light from rainbow [Sketch of 7 Yods in arc]

"Spirit of Primal Fire"

21 [Tau] UNIVERSE: Wreath of 12 big and 72 small circles. Woman, scarf, legs crossed Wands in hands, one down one up, luna crescent on head.

Heptagram in woman

Kerubim round   Man   Eagle

                     Ox   Lion

[Sketch of circle with Heptagram and four Kerubim names in position as text]

"The Great one of the Night and Time"

With these images of the twenty-two Major Arcana in our mind, as would have been placed within Golden Dawn ceremonies, we can lay out a Tree of Life and see how these might variously illustrate the nature of every aspect of the Tree. We will first look at several reasons why we should utilise this system and learn correspondences for our spiritual work.

The Tarot and Tree of Life

The Tree of Life diagram was not notably taken out of its original Judaic context until the first translation of *Gates of Light* in 1516. The tarot, meanwhile, arose in its acceptably recognised format and structure in the earlier 15th century. This actually dates the origination of the tarot structure **prior** to common knowledge of the Kabbalah, although the Kabbalah itself had been developed for many centuries prior – there being evidence of the *Sepher Yetzirah* being in existence by the 10th Century.[12] There are no historical records of their connection until the supposition made by Comte de Mellet and Court de Gébelin in 1781.

After Etteilla's work in popularising the tarot as cartomancy, the first author to then significantly develop the connection between the two systems of tarot and Kabbalah was Eliphas Levi (1810-1875) who utilised the tarot as a convenient filing system for his esoteric ideas and as chapter sections in his books. This utilisation was taken up even more explicitly by Aleister Crowley (1875-1947), whose poetry, shorter pieces of fiction, Holy Books, and other works are often structured upon the Tree of Life – verses of 10 or 22 lines, keyphrases, paragraphs structured on the elements, can all be seen to be based on correspondences.

So the first use we have in learning the correspondences between tarot and the Tree of Life is for a simple utilitarian and practical reason – it is so we can read and understand the writings of those who have gone before us on the path of the Western Esoteric Initiatory System. The Kabbalah is one of the languages which they learnt, spoke and in which they wrote, so we cannot pretend to understand their writing if we do not even know the language in which it was written.

That was the first piece of esoteric advice I ever received, from a man called Andy, the owner of the Ace of Wands bookshop in

---

[12] Scholem, G. *Kabbalah*, p.23.

Derby, when I wandered into his shop as a spotty teenager in the early 1980's and tried to load myself up with books by Crowley, Fortune, Regardie and Anton LaVey. He laughed, pointed me back to the shelves, and had me pick up instead a beginners book on Yoga, and a beginner's book on Kabbalah. He said to me:

"You'll be better learning what they learnt first, then reading what they wrote".

That was the first sentence I ever heard from a teacher and now I pass it on – learn some of the language first, experience some of the exercises first, and it will be much easier in the long-term. There are many other good reasons to learn the correspondences, some of which will become more obvious as your experience develops, but in the meantime, we will look at the primary reasons.

Why Learn the Correspondences?

The Tree of Life and the tarot do not arise in nature outside of us; the *Sephiroth* do not exist in the same way that a cloud exists, nor for that matter, does love. The archetype drawn as the Empress on a card does not exist in the same way that a river or a mountain exist; nor even is she the same as a real Empress. The word Empress does not exist in the same way to that which it signifies; a real woman sat on a real chair, given authority over some land or another. In fact, the word Empress is not the same as the same word in Bosnian or Bulgarian, Arabic or Cantonese.

In addition to that, when we look at a mountain, a river, the object of our love or a cloud floating in the sky above a Bosnian landscape, we do not truly know what we are observing. It depends on our own state at the time – most importantly – and our senses. A dolphin will not look up and see that cloud in the way we do, neither will a telescope. However, both the dolphin and the scientist looking through a telescope may fall in love with the cloud, in their own particular and peculiar manner.

The world arises for us in our experience, and our experience shares some commonality; in language, in the archetypal patterns, in the form of a spiral that we all agree is the shape of a shell, an unfolding fern leaf or a galaxy – even the water draining from our bath agrees to conform and with our notion of a spiral.

And with that concept of a spiral, we make further observations; we see deeper patterns, perhaps. We see that often life is like a spiral in other ways; we appear to go around in circles and return to something we have done before, only now we ourselves have moved on, we see the same thing differently. Or perhaps we feel that we are spiralling downwards instead; into debt, into addiction, into disaster, just like the bath water. Or perhaps we realise we can never step in the same river twice, even though there is no real river, nor are we stepping into it.

But having these ideas, seeing these patterns, we can observe more fully, we can realise things about our engagement with the universe that we may not have previously seen, and we can learn – and act differently in future. We can use our awareness of these fundamental patterns arising out of the interface apparently between our self and the universe to shape our reality in a very practical sense, test them, and find the limits of our existence.[13] This is the Great Work.

By making a correspondence between two systems or more, we increase our ability to recognise, incorporate and utilise these universal patterns, and in so doing we further the Great Work. In fact, by making correspondence, we also get to elicit the patterns, through invocation and evocation and other mechanisms of truly engaging life, not escaping it.

---

[13] The interface is seen as the Veil of *Paroketh* on the Tree of Life when considered as the interaction of self and existence, and as the Abyss on the Tree when considered as the interaction of self and the divine. There is no interface between the divine and existence, nor ultimately, any interface at all.

Why Tarot? Why Kabbalah?

The test of any correspondence system is its ability to model reality as we experience it. It should be able to diagnose and predict events and demonstrate comprehensiveness, congruity and consistency to experience. If I am in a business meeting and there are three other people, all of whom are very different yet seem to be working very well together, I might expect to discover that they correspond to three of the four Court Cards in tarot or three of the classical Elements. This will further tell me that I should draw upon the fourth "missing" element to best fit into the meeting.[14]

It can be said that unless we have a model – or part of one - we cannot expect to observe its pattern in our perception. I recall first learning about "force-field analysis" during a business diploma, whilst being engaged in my first management role. I suddenly "saw" the events playing out around me in terms of force-field analysis, between team members, different teams in the company, and between the company and its competition. Whilst I would have been vaguely aware of these events, the model gave me a pair of glasses which brought them into distinct focus, rather than the vague blur of uninformed sight or total ignorance. There are many models and systems that when you see the world through them, they can change your entire awareness and resultant behaviour, whether for business or mysticism.

The Kabbalah and tarot have stabilised into reasonably structured systems over centuries of experience. As the Kabbalists say, "ten and not nine, ten and not eleven".[15] The tarot is universally recognised as a common structure of 22 Major Arcana, and 4 Suits, with 10 Minor cards and 4 Court Cards in each Suit. These find

---

[14] This is drawn from real experience and is not an idle example. There are a lot of business plans in my own past that are now in the archives of private or public companies, from industry to education, that have 10 section headings and 22 sub-sections, in 4 parts.

[15] Matt, D. C. *The Essential Kabbalah*, p. 76

immediate correspondence to the 22 Hebrew letters, the 4 Worlds, and the 10 *Sephiroth* of the Tree of Life by their basic structure.

It is as if when we go exploring the world, no matter where we start and what we do, we find almost the same thing is underneath – or above it – all. Something incomprehensible, which we then model in exactly the same way, no matter the language.

We could equally use Chakras, the I-Ching or the Runes, for example, as part of our correspondence system, however, the further we culturally remove ourselves from our own history, the more difficult it may be to map correspondences for the time we have and the practical usage it will give us.

There are sufficient correspondences for a lifetime of study and appreciation in the tarot and the Kabbalah; although we may extend that quite quickly to astrology, herbalism, classical divinities, colour symbolism, numerology, and other systems that are woven into the Neo-Platonic, Hermetic or Gnostic garments worn by the tradition.

We will now look at the reason for different systems and then go on to look at the core correspondences. In further chapters we will unpack and explore the several different of the most fundamental correspondence systems.

Why Different Correspondence Systems?

An often off-putting aspect of esoteric is the currency placed on correspondence systems, and their validity against some notion of truth. The "one true system" is often the one "most secret" and revealed only to an "exalted grade", until a member of that grade leaves their Order in some conflict and publishes it for everyone to see. It then appears that the system is only a variation on a theme.

I was taught originally that truth was a measure of the usefulness of an idea in practice. I could believe it "true" that I could fly, but it would not be a particularly useful notion if my Will was to live a long life, and I tested that belief from the top of a tall building. The instruction I was given along with that concept of truth was "test everything". A far more practical philosophy than most, such considerations soon drive the practitioner to the most useful models and maps for their experience.

Each correspondence system is just such a map and just a model, as we have already described. And like maps, we can have a whole range of maps of the same location, each useful for different journeys.

When I am looking for a map of London, where I am going to drive to visit my son, I look for a map that shows the streets, the one-way systems, and the current traffic diversions. I do not look for a map of the same place that shows its variations in temperature, geography, or contours.

However, if I were considering walking around a place, I would want a more granular or detailed map – of the same place – and perhaps even one that showed contours.

If I were a wheelchair user, I might require another layer on that map, not necessarily required by others making the same journey. If I am just going into London for a night out, a little pamphlet with a humorous cartoon map of the "Best Pub Crawl in London" would probably suffice until the following day.

It is exactly the same with the correspondence systems of the Tree of Life, that different stages of the spiritual or life journey, different purposes, and different states of being require different maps. Those maps are all illustrating the same place – our engagement with the Universe – but marked differently for different types of journey.

It is only when we mistake the map for the territory, as a "real thing" with "validity" that we could even think of arguing that "System X" is "better" than "System Y". To the Adept, that discussion would never even arise as a possibility. It is not even that one system is "better" than another; the systems are maps, not the thing being mapped.

So the Golden Dawn system of correspondences, drawn from various sources, hung upon the Tree of Life in a particular pattern, is useful for those working through the GD system; and for those practising magick in general, from its generally Hermetic, Gnostic and Neo-Platonic sources.

The system as modified by Crowley, to switch the Emperor and the Star between the paths marked *Heh* and *Tzaddi*, is useful for those who align with Crowley's reception of the *Book of the Law*. Although, it is notable that even Crowley forgot later about his switch, when he wrote about the Emperor card in his *Book of Thoth*.

The Waite-Trinick system of correspondences, which is a more major (if you'll pardon the pun) variation on the Golden Dawn system, is more useful, in my mind, to those following the considerations of a peculiarly Christian esotericism above the grade of *Adeptus Minor*. It is at that point that the reasons for holding a magical map become obsolete and redundant.

There are other variations; Charles Stansfeld-Jones (1886–1950) turned the correspondences upside-down, and later, so did William G. Gray (1913–1992). Neither of these systems received a particularly wide-spread attention or take-up into whatever passes for mainstream esotericism. Another alternate system is proposed by Paul Roland (2005) and there are many more if you go searching for them online.

In tarot, the correspondence of Major Arcana to the letters of the Hebrew Alphabet and hence to the Tree of Life will mainly depend on whether we place the unnumbered Fool at the beginning or end of the sequence, or even prior to the World card as in some variations. Similarly, the correspondence of the Court Cards to Astrology receives variant treatment according to which version of Astrology one might be considering. It will also depend on whether we place *Da'ath* on the Tree of Life or not, and whether we have three or one paths connecting *Malkuth* to the Tree.

The important thing is the doctrine itself; the principle of correspondence – and its primary purpose, which is to create a state of mind in which all things are interconnected in a pattern beyond observation, imagination, thought or attachment – one that ultimately arises in awareness as a simple unity. We do not get lost in disagreements about someone else's illusion, as the map is a part of the territory, and further, it lies within the territory.

In summary, then, we have different systems for different purposes – my recommendation is the same as was given to me, to learn one, and test its usefulness. If you do not test your map against your experience, you will never realise that you are a long way away from the destination it describes to those who do make the journey.

We will next look at two of the primary systems of correspondence (Golden Dawn and Waite-Trinick) used within the Order of Everlasting Day and note several of the further variations for your exploration. These maps can be further explored in astral travel, dream-work, ritual, and by other means in addition to mapping everyday experience.[16]

However, before we look at the systems, we will provide the basic meanings of the *Sephiroth* on the Tree. We will then later in the book look at the paths themselves. In this way we can build our knowledge and experience of the Tree in stages.

The Sephiroth
The Kabbalistic model of the universe, most often depicted as the Tree of Life is composed of ten *Sephiroth*. Whilst these are commonly drawn as circles, sometimes simply as ten concentric circles, more often as ten circles connected by the twenty-two Paths, they are not simply circles. A common mistake in many

---

[16] See Katz, M. *The Magister*, Vol. 1 (forthcoming, 2016).

books is to refer to them as "spheres" but the term is **not** related to the Greek word for 'sphere'.[17] In fact, it is closer in relation to the Hebrew word for 'sapphire', which reflects the radiant nature of the divine.

A number of other synonyms are used for the *Sephiroth*; "sayings", "names", "lights", "powers", "stages", even "garments", "mirrors" and "shoots". The *Zohar* refers to them also as "aspects".[18]

Whatever they are called, they are ten aspects of the Universe, each with their own qualities and nature. When they are arranged together, they function as an entire engine of divine creation.

For ongoing reference, the list below gives the most simple name and general significance of each of the ten *Sephiroth* on the Tree of Life as they are usually seen in Kabbalah.[19]

> 1. Kether – the crown of the Tree, the divine source and singular point of all creation.
>
> 2. Chockmah – the force of the Tree, the male energy.
>
> 3. Binah – the form of the Tree, the female energy.▯
>
> 4. Chesed – the expansive nature of creation, love and mercy.
>
> 5. Geburah – the constraining nature of creation, fear and severity.
>
> 6. Tiphareth – the harmonizing point in the centre of all things, the self.

---

[17] Scholem, G. *Kabbalah*, p. 99.
[18] *Ibid*, p. 100.
[19] These are extremely simplified and are expanded in later chapters. I also recommend Schulman, Y. D. *The Sefirot* as a reference guide to their various meanings.

7. Netzach – the natural cycles of eternal creation and nature, the emotions.

8. Hod – the definition of things into formation, the structure of the mind, analysis.

9. Yesod – the foundation of existence, the unconscious, the psyche and personality, dreams and images.

10. Malkuth – the world as it actually is, unknowable other than through Yesod, our perceptions.

The actual spelling and literal meanings of the titles are as follows:

Sephirah	Hebrew	Translations (most common word given first in bold)
Kether	KThR	**Crown**, diadem, to surround, besiege, wait, encompass
Chockmah	ChKMH	**Wisdom**, experience, knowledge, intelligence, insight, judgement, science, midwife
Binah	BYNH	**Understanding**, insight, prudence, reason, discernment
Da'ath	DA'aTh	**Knowledge**, insight, wisdom, understanding

Chesed	ChSD	**Mercy**, grace, piety, beauty, good-will, favour, benefit, love, kindness, charity, righteousness, benevolence, to do good
Geburah	GBVRH	**Strength**, power, force, valour, courage, victory, might, God, hero
Tiphareth	ThPhARTh	**Beauty**, splendour, magnificence, ornament, honour, glory, boast
Netzach	NTzCh	**Victory,** splendour, glory, truth, power, firmness, confidence, eminence. Duration, perpetuity, eternity, lasting, enduring. To excel, be superior, strength, blood, to be chief. Music-master, precentor, to sparkle, shine, win.
Hod	HVD	**Glory**, splendour, majesty, renown, ornament, beauty
Yesod	YSVD	**Foundation**, base, ground, principle, compilation

Malkuth	MLKVTh	**Kingdom**, dominion, realm, reign

We will now look at how the Golden Dawn laid out a schema of initiation based on these concepts, arranged upon the Tree of Life. In essence, they took the approach that if the Tree of Life showed the ten stages of creation, our return to the divine would take exactly the same ten stages, in the same order, back up the Tree of Life. In contemporary terms, this is referred to as an ascent narrative. This ascent is a purely intellectual and spiritual, resulting in initiatory change. It is described in one traditional Kabbalistic book, the *Sefer ha-Tzeruf*, as "when the sphere of the intellect is moved by the Agent Intellect and the person begins to enter it and to ascend the sphere which returns, like the image of a ladder, and at the time of the ascent his thoughts shall be really transformed and all the visions shall be changed before him, and there will be nothing left to him of what he had earlier."[20]

The Golden Dawn System

The Golden Dawn system originates from the Cipher manuscripts likely created by Kenneth McKenzie (1833 – 1886) and developed by the founders of the Order, S. L. Macgregor Mathers (1854 – 1918), W. W. Westcott (1848 – 1925) and W. R. Woodman (1828 – 1891), in 1888. The system follows the Tree of Life diagram according to Kircher (1602 – 1680), which has three paths connecting *Malkuth* and no split paths into *Da'ath* as used by some models. It is Kircher's diagram, published in his erroneous work on Egyptology, *Oedipus Aegyptiacus* (1653), with its extensive tables and wheels of correspondences that is the source for the most-used version of the Tree of Life in esotericism.[21] The Cipher manuscript does include a sketch of the Tree of Life with the paths split by

---

[20] Quoted in Idel, M. *Ascensions on High in Jewish Mysticism*, p. 39.
[21] See http://billheidrick.com/Orpd/AKir/AKOeAell.htm [last accessed 24th May 2015]

Da'ath, and there is a sketch in unpublished archive papers (see later) but this was not apparently utilised until Waite's F.R.C. version – nor was it utilised by Crowley.

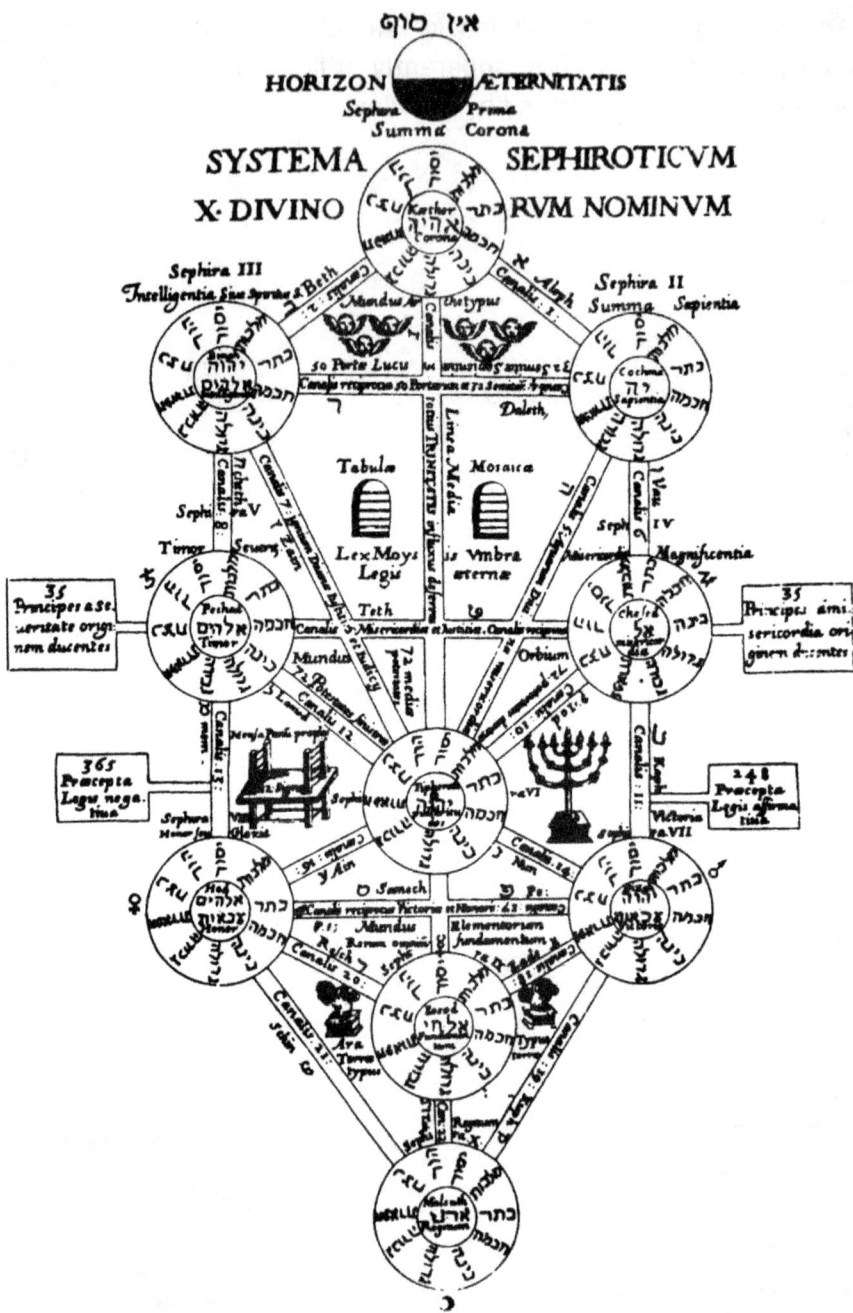

Illus. Tree of Life from Kircher, Oedipus Aegyptiacus (1653).

The description of the correspondences is given in these Cipher manuscripts in the "Knowledge of the Practicus" grade, and follows a sequence of the Hebrew letters, path numbers, and then the correspondence of the tarot. Interestingly, the Fool is numbered "1" as is the Magician, and the sequence is written with Strength as 11 and Justice as 8, but then manually changed with two lines crossing the cards over.

Whilst the cards and their correspondences are not listed in a particular sequence in the cipher, they are presented in the Order according to their Hebrew letter order or their numerical card order.

Here are the correspondences as given in the Golden Dawn System.

Letter	Path on Tree	Connecting Sephiroth	Tarot Correspondence	Astrological Correspondence
Aleph	11	1-2	0 : FOOL	Air
Beth	12	1-3	I : MAGICIAN	Mercury
Gimel	13	1-6	II : PRIESTESS	Moon
Daleth	14	2-3	III : EMPRESS	Venus
Heh	15	2-6	IV : EMPORER	Aries
Vau	16	2-4	V : HIEROPHANT	Taurus
Zain	17	3-6	VI : LOVERS	Gemini
Cheth	18	3-5	VII : CHARIOT	Cancer
Teth	19	4-5	VIII : STRENGTH	Leo

Yod	20	4-6	IX : HERMIT	Virgo
Kaph	21	4-7	X : WHEEL	Jupiter
Lamed	22	5-6	XI : JUSTICE	Libra
Mem	23	5-8	XII : HANGED MAN	Water
Nun	24	6-7	XIII : DEATH	Scorpio
Samekh	25	6-9	XIV : TEMPERANCE	Sagittarius
Ayin	26	6-8	XV : DEVIL	Capricorn
Peh	27	7-8	XVI : TOWER	Mars
Tzaddi	28	7-9	XVII : STAR	Aquarius
Qoph	29	7-10	XVIII : MOON	Pisces
Resh	30	8-9	XIX : SUN	Sun
Shin	31	8-10	XX : LAST JUDGEMENT	Fire
Tau	32	9-10	XXI : UNIVERSE	Saturn/Earth

In the Golden Dawn system, the Astrological correspondences are allocated according to the division within the Hebrew language itself. The Hebrew letters are divided into three "Mother" letters, seven "Double" letters, and twelve "Single" letters as follows:

Mother Letters: שמא

Double Letters: תרפכדגב

Single Letters: קצעסליטחזוה

To the Mother letters are allocated the three elements of Air, Fire and Water. The Double letters have the seven visible planets attributed to them, and the twelve Single letters have the constellations of the Zodiac attributed to them. The Element of Earth is allocated to Tau with the planet Saturn.

The cards were presented to initiates during ritual, drawn crudely onto large boards and fastened onto stands which would likely be moved about the temple. In our research to date, no actual images have been found above the Death card in reverse sequence, i.e. no images exist for cards 1 - 14 or the 0, although at least one list of text descriptions exists, as given previously. The Death card would have been the last card to be required by the Outer Order ceremonies.

There is new evidence to suggest that other slightly later temples did draw full decks, and this is presently under research.[22]

In a similar way, no coloured images of the cards for the Waite-Trinick images for the upper part of the Tree exist to our knowledge. This appears to demonstrate how the images in both cases were a work-in-progress and both were unfortunately interrupted before their completion.[23]

---

[22] As at 25th May 2015, please see www.tarotassociation.net for any future updates.
[23] Katz, M. & Goodwin, T. *Abiding in the Sanctuary*.

The Grades of the Golden Dawn

In our discussion of the Western Esoteric Initiatory System (WEIS) we will refer to the grades of initiation within the Golden Dawn and other Orders. These grades are the steps of magical and spiritual ascent mapped onto the Tree of Life and each have a specific title, drawn from a German magical order, the Gold and Rosy Cross, a century prior to the Golden Dawn.[24] We give those titles here for reference with a brief indication of their nature in the Order of Everlasting Day.

---

[24] See Katz, M. *The Magister, Vol 0.*

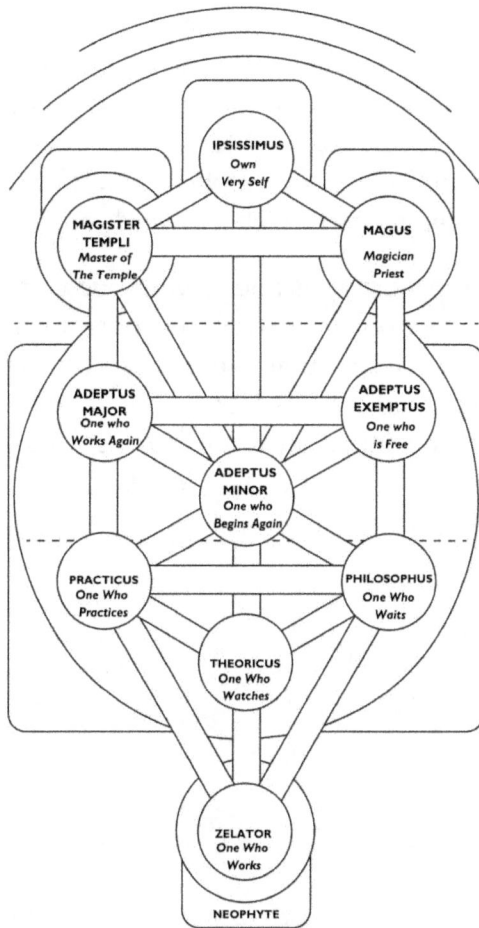

Illus. Grades of Initiation on the Tree of Life.

The Tree of the Golden Dawn

In terms of initiatory progress, the map given by the Golden Dawn, illustrated by the tarot, is partially explained within the Order rituals themselves, which have since been widely published. These descriptions were presented up to the point of the Death card, and only sketched out in the remaining cards as "inner order" secrets. As in much that is truly esoteric, the words on paper, the descriptions spoken in a temple, cannot convey the actual experience and learning of which the words are mere description.

If we consider the journey as one in which we visit the ten *Sephiroth* on the Tree, and from each can look both up and down to our previous and next destination, we can see the tarot as illustrating challenges ahead and lessons learnt. This is an important concept which we teach beginners in tarot courses; to see each card as a challenge and lesson. It prepares tarot beginners who might later wish to study the WEIS.

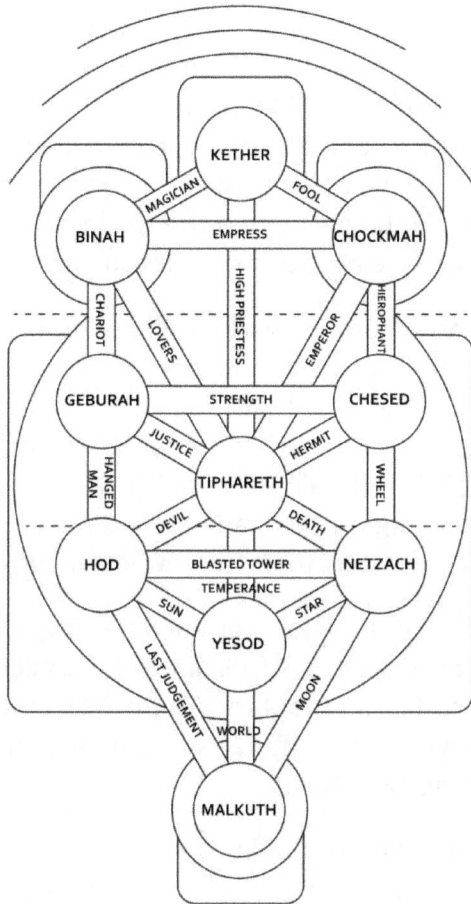

Illus. Tarot Cards on the Tree of Life (Golden Dawn System).

1. Malkuth.

Here we stand at the beginning of our journey, as a Zelator of the Order. It is our first significant step (after the Neophyte grade) into working with esoteric philosophy and practice. We have no prior lessons, we only see ahead of us three challenges; the World, the Last Judgement and the Moon. These three images together illustrate a key statement in the Neophyte ritual; "the light shineth in the darkness, but the darkness comprehendeth it not". The Moon reflects the light of the divine into the world, and we rise from our eternal sleep when we answer a distant calling from above.

The challenges are clear; the world itself and all its attachments and distractions being the main problem. How do we 'escape' the mundane world? How do we 'fit' the esoteric into this world? How will it change the way we look at our world – and make changes to that world? Is the world all we have? Is it enough? These are all questions that belong on this path, sometimes called the "path of the terrible Tau", referring to its Hebrew letter correspondence.

There is fear too about the journey ahead – we see this in the Moon card. There is also a sense of distance, impossibility, the blurred lines between reality and fantasy. There is even the beginning of the splitting between our natural and our civilised sides, between our wild and domestic selves.

Yet into this illustration of our life we have risen to meet a call, no matter how much grave dirt we will come to dig. All aspects of our self; male, female, child, have responded to this calling – and we begin to reach up, albeit blindly, to something more than ourselves.

There is a trap here; the Moon reflects everything that is shone upon it, the World is full of itself. We can become trapped here in reflections of our own projections, believing we are making progress and congratulating ourselves endlessly on how well we are doing, how safe we have become in our success in the world – whether mundane, magical, mystical or spiritual.

In a sense too, we never leave these paths, the process is cumulative, as if we are building a whole engine from each of these parts, or a house upon these foundations. The Golden Dawn state that the lower grades "quit not Malkuth" and we must constantly return to this map to ensure we have not gone astray.

A person at this grade can be easily recognised – as any grade – by their state, actions and most importantly the questions they are presenting the world, spoken - or by their behaviour, which in itself is only an enquiry into the nature of their engagement with the universe. The questions any human is asking by their speech and activity are the only relevant and true indicator of their progress in the quest, as those questions demonstrate what has not yet been exhausted by their Work. And all questions speak of One who questions and Another which answers. Transcendence, then, is merely the pure exhaustion of all questions and all separation.

A person at this grade will be busy, constantly doing new things; they will be delighted with each discovery as if it is of major significance. They will be testing their limits – and the limits of those around them. They will be excitable, keen to tell you about the world, yet often failing overall to meet their ambitions, and constantly unsatisfied. They will be ambitious, active and keen, even if quietly. They will judge themselves by others, and the world around them, not any internal measure.

Their constant questions can all be seen as flavours of one simple enquiry; "What can I do to distract me from my death". This is the lowest question and the perversion of the question of the Adept.

All of this and much more can be seen in those three card illustrations. They represent a perfect map of human behaviour on the spiritual journey, one that applies to any tradition, and time, and any person. This is the power of the WEIS to model initiatory progress.

The escape from this state is not present in the illustrations, as it must be initiated by someone else, someone outside of you. This is unavoidable and whilst the concept of hierarchy and teaching is often dismissed in the "New Age" beliefs of becoming your own saviour, and not following others, it is something that remains true by any observation.

Many people spend their whole lives merely becoming better and better Zelators.

2. Yesod

When we are at last uplifted from our state in *Malkuth* to *Yesod* by another, one who watches us asleep and chooses to awaken us, we have our first opportunity to look back and see the world differently. In fact, we look at the map and see it is indeed the World tarot card that is now "below" us. We have attained a new state, a new perspective, a new outlook for the very first time. We have been initiated and the World is a different place.

Whilst we are still "cradled" in the paths illustrated by Judgement and the Moon, we now also have access to the paths of the Sun and Star either side of us, and the Temperance card above us.

The first observation is that having shifted our state, we have an Angel above us, not the World. We may feel more spiritually connected, but this is a trap again – our connection is to our "Self" centre not to the divine. Immediately many practitioners get a sense that having accomplished one significant state-change, they have become enlightened above others. They become overwhelmed by a more direct connection to their inner world, and aggrandise themselves through exposure to its limitless content. They immediately begin to talk with their own "higher self", "inner self", "angel", "guide", or somesuch and this fixes them in their place and starts to feed upon them.

Or they become prophets for their cause, speaking to everyone of the path they are upon, and how wonderful, exalted and incredible it all is, if only others could see it.

The challenge, again, given in the card illustrations, is simple; Temperance.

We have to balance the light of awareness (Sun) and our sense of Will (Star) to constantly try and stay awake in the knowledge that "every man and every woman is a star". We will continue to go round the same habitual cycles (Moon) and keep deciding to do differently next time (Last Judgement), and this may cause despair and disillusionment (Sun and Star reversed).

But the work is going on regardless (Temperance) – a true "Tempering" of the ego/self-identity process in constant motion. This is intimated in our map by the Blasted Tower being the next level up; it connects *Hod* and *Netzach* yet is not yet accessed by the Practitioner other than its influence through *Hod* and *Netzach* on *Yesod*.

3. Hod
The way out of *Yesod* is through the path of the Sun. It is a direct allusion to the *Sephirah Tiphareth*, which also corresponds to the Sun after another manner. In the practice given to the Theoricus in *Yesod*, they eventually break through into a new constant state which is sudden, immediate and dramatic. In this we see the impact of the Blasted Tower, as it often happens together with significant change in the outer life of the initiate. It can for many be the first experience of a "magical" event paralleling a "mundane" event.

In *Hod* we have now passed the path of the Sun card, so we have "mastered" it, or more technically, "utilised" it so its main purpose is redundant, other than as a reminder. You cannot go backwards from this point, although at any grade you can remain and stagnate.

This is the first experience too where we have access to a path that goes across the veil on the Tree of Life. The path of the Hanged Man indicates the overturning of consciousness that is being experienced, and challenges us further to the idea of sacrifice and living to our highest values. Again, this is an intimation of *Tiphareth*, for which all four lower grades are preparation.

We also see from *Hod* the paths of the Devil and Blasted Tower. We can test our attachments to the world and our old sense of self, but this will only take us up a path for which we cannot pass. We must exhaust ourselves of our Devil, there is no beating him. Then we walk across the path of the Tower, in a constant building up, testing and destruction of our beliefs about ourselves.

On the map, we see how this crosses (literally) Temperance, reminding us of the constant alchemy and balance required as we destroy ourselves.

The initiate here can often experience highs and lows, as they oscillate on the tightrope path with *Yesod* below and *Tiphareth* below, yet no direct connection to either *Sephirah*. This is the worst of all times for most on the path, alternate dry periods, struggles, petty gains and losses. The questions they will ask all boil down to "What is this worth?"

4. Netzach

In *Netzach*, we have respite from the Blasted Tower whose path, whilst still active in our life, we have passed across to a resting place. We have learnt the limits of thought and logic, and consolidated (for now) our philosophy of life, to simply begin living it.

We find ourselves being able to look down the paths of the Star and Moon, perhaps even allowing ourselves a moment to wryly grin at the ignorance of our fears when we first started this journey, and the stupidity of our former hopes and wishes.

We experience here stability in motion; the Star and Moon have their orbits, the rumbles of the Blasted Tower are in the past, and now we look to see the Wheel reaching through the veil. Our life becomes part of a larger cycle; we integrate ourselves to nature in its fullest sense, and begin the process of surrendering to life. It is with no irony that the Death card illustrates our portal here to *Tiphareth*.

When the initiate has traversed and exhausted all the strategies of the lower paths, and experienced the *Sephirah* to *Netzach*, they ask the same question in a thousand ways; "What else is there?"

5. Tiphareth

Tiphareth is the grand central station of the Tree and as such, the meeting place for many journeys and often their final destination – or simply the commencement of a whole new journey. In the four worlds model of the Tree of Life, where four trees are overlapped to form "Jacob's Ladder", *Tiphareth* is from where each subsequent Tree "grows". So it becomes the point of resonance and a wormhole between the dimensions of each Tree. This is beyond our current work here, but described in more detail in *The Magister*. The Four Worlds model is a very detailed refinement of the general model, allowing us to specifically predict nuances of state in the journey, such as boredom, desperation, excitement, obsession, and any other state of human existence. It also allows us to map increasingly rarefied and abstract states of mystical experience.

In just one Tree, we see on our map that *Tiphareth* is a major landmark. In the Order of the Golden Dawn and many other Orders, it is the grade in which we enter an "Inner Order" of a very different nature to the Outer Order of the lower *Sephiroth*.

It is no surprise then to see that it is Death that leads us into *Tiphareth*; it is the death and transformation of all previous states and senses of self-identity. These are presented on the pyre of sacrifice in *Tiphareth* and utterly undone. In fact, once the Adept grade is taken here, we must return to all previous states of our being and "redeem" them. This is included in the instruction manual of the WEIS by the word "recapitulation"; we have to go back through our life and contextualise it again in the light of our new state of disattachment. All those experiences were preparation – we have to revisit them and utterly understand for what we were being prepared.

In *Tiphareth*, as we see, the High Priestess illustrates the path that leads directly to the most highest of *Sephirah*; *Kether*, the Crown, the point of divinity and total illumination. The Adept recognises some of this in their experience, but the Abyss that is shown on the map is suddenly experienced; there is some critical and profound division or distance between ourselves and the divine, no matter what we do.

As it becomes obvious that we cannot simply walk into enlightenment, for now, we look around and see that we have the paths of Justice and the Hermit streaming down to us, and the Lovers and the Emperor reaching down to us from higher up the Tree.

Yet we cannot move on until we have released ourselves from the Death and Devil paths below us. They support us, for sure, yet they are also chains that hold us back. In a sense too is the Temperance path that once served us so well.

In this state, so powerful yet so lost, once our previous life has been utterly gathered up and we have no need of it – or anything – there is only one possible route. We must call upon high for an Angel to guide us. Nothing else will serve us, as everything else is below the veil to us now. If we returned to it, we would soon be lost again and dissatisfied. We have tasted a brief moment of transcendence, and now we fear that we may always have to live with what life is like without it.

The Abramelin Operation of the WEIS is the means and method by which we remove ourselves from life and our self, and gain the knowledge and conversation of our Holy Guardian Angel. This incorporates and utilises the paths of Death and the Devil in a six-month spiritual-magical practice of intense devotion and self-destruction. If the work has not been done properly of the previous journey, it is futile and the Adept risks everything in its attempt. To fail is to completely undo any chance of future progress through this system.

The Adept will face the challenges of temptation (Lovers) and power (Emperor) in this work, both of which arise from attachment.

When freed from attachment, they become divine intuition and open channelling of energy. Similarly, the High Priestess is the challenge of the illusion of light, when what we must come to see is the source of the light, not be blinded by it.

The only question that matters to the Adept is "What is Death?"

6. Geburah

This first of the higher grades beyond *Adeptus Minor* in *Tiphareth* is one of construction and structure, discipline and management. It brings about the responsibilities of creating a structure in which teaching can take place. The Work moves from learning to teaching-as-learning.

The lesson learnt is that of the Hanged Man, the *Adeptus Major* here has learnt about sacrifice and transcended the necessity of such sacrifice. Above them is the Chariot card, which in the Thoth Tarot is an empty suit of armour; someone who has entirely emptied themselves (like the Grail) to the divine influence. The second path leading out below *Geburah* is illustrated by the Justice card, showing how the adept must come to balance their life as a whole, whilst remaining in a state of non-attachment.

Whereas the first journey across the Tree of Life between the two pillars was marked by the Blasted Tower card, this second transition out of *Geburah* is marked by Strength. The Adept must create a dynamic union between their own life and the life of their Angel.

At this point there are few outward questions, other than "How do I communicate" but perhaps the internalised question is "How do I remain alive?"

7. Chesed

Whilst all are equal, perhaps we can see this way-station as one of the most unique and critical on the Tree of Life. It is here that we come to the edge of the Abyss that marks the division between human awareness in totality and divine annihilation. There is no "separate" being above the Abyss, so there is little that can be said of the three primary states that reside above it.

The Hierophant illustrates the path now open to this stage of the journey, who reveals at last the sacred union that awaits the Adept. Below us in only time, streaming forth and cycling in the Wheel card and all things are one in that unceasing rotation. The Hermit is our image for the connection we now make back to what once passed as "self". We are no longer following the way; we have become the way, the light and the truth of the moment in pure experience.

It is here for the first time that our map appears to fail us, for there is no direct path from our position in *Chesed* to the next numerical *Sephirah*, *Binah*, which awaits us on the other side of the Abyss. However, this is a fundamental representation of the journey at this higher stage; there is no direct path, there is only the leap of faith, the letting go of all accomplishment that opens the world of the final three *Sephiroth*.

8. Binah
On the other side of the Abyss, where the three *Sephiroth* function as one unified triad, we can only guess as to what is illustrated by the cards. In the WEIS, the title of the grade here in *Binah* is Master of the Temple, that Temple being the universe.

The Empress connects the position of *Binah* to *Chockmah*, and in the Golden Dawn this card was seen as significant to the concept of "unity" and "love" through its correspondence to Venus, the only planetary symbol which when drawn on the Tree of Life connected all the *Sephiroth*.

So we can presume that an understanding (the literal translation of *Binah*) of unity is paramount to the work of this space.

Our path here down back to selfhood is that of the Lovers, showing that we still have a choice to leave this garden, and fall back down to a separate sense of self. This is something that Crowley warns about in his tract about the "black brothers", when the initiate "secretes his elements about his ego" as if he could remain separate to the Universe.

Above us is the final path to unity, the crown of *Kether*, the end of our journey, marked as we might expect by the Magician card – the supreme attainment of magick, then, is this state. We still exist, in a sense, but there is only the channelling of what is above to that which is below, and all the elements are placed before us for our service.

The final path leading below from *Binah* is that of the Chariot. Now we see the emptiness that was first glimpsed in the fearful position of *Geburah* – yet we cannot be afraid, for we are no longer.

9. Chockmah
Having attained the grade of Magus, according to Crowley the task now is to create the Universe to Will – a will now aligned with every aspect of existence. There is no separation here, but to attain the final state, the Magus must destroy all duality of act, word and thought.

This is clearly illustrated in the three paths that lead from *Chockmah* below:

> Empress: Duality of Action
>
> Emperor: Duality of Word
>
> Hierophant: Duality of Thought

These three cards of temporal, worldly and spiritual power illustrate the three final temptations that might keep the Magus from voluntarily surrendering everything.

10. Kether
Finally, the crown is attained and we enter into true enlightenment. The final path of the Fool that connects *Kether* to *Chockmah* illustrates this final leap into spiritual bliss and freedom.

We are now both Magician and High Priestess, the channel of the divine and its light. There is nothing now for us to do, for we have become the doing, the Zero, the Fool.

We have now concluded our commentary on the Tree of Life and tarot correspondences according to the Golden Dawn system. However, we now turn our attention to an alternate model published here in for the first time and provide accompanying commentary. Whilst the Tree of Life was seen as above in the "natural order" of the paths, there was a sketch model within the original Golden Dawn documents that provided a variant system of correspondences. This was based on a different way of arranging the paths on the Tree and the inclusion of *Da'ath*. It may well have been this alternate model that provided A. E. Waite an inspiration for his own system as we will come to examine shortly.

Whilst there is no commentary on this variant to the "natural" arrangement, we may assume that with the inclusion of *Da'ath* that it represents the unnatural or native state of the Tree of Life after the Fall – and ourselves likewise. In several other diagrams within the Order and as presented within the rituals we see this two-state model presented; the Garden of Eden before the Fall (to which we aspire to return) and the Garden after the Fall, in which state the candidate is within as they commence their journey.

So let us briefly look at this unnatural arrangement of the Tree and point out several illustrations within it that show us our unredeemed nature.

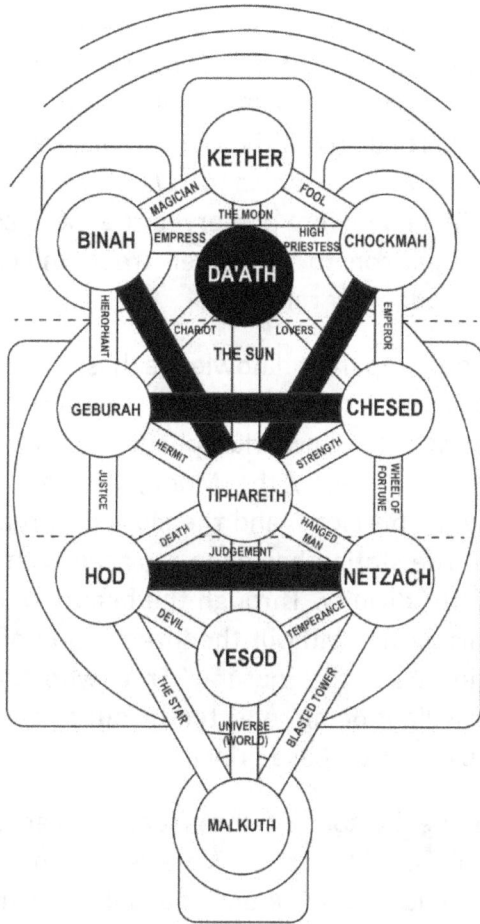

Illus. Tarot Cards on Tree of Life (Golden Dawn System with Da'ath).

The Tree of Night Before the Dawn

In this Tree, we immediately see that the placing of *Da'ath* upon the map has broken several paths and created new paths, particularly those two now connecting it with *Geburah* and *Chesed*. The paths connecting *Tiphareth* to *Binah* and *Chockmah* are removed, as is the path between *Hod* and *Netzach*. This gives the Tree a more lattice arrangement – particularly in the original diagram where the paths between *Da'ath* and *Binah* and *Chockmah* are drawn at a downward angle. I have here preserved the more common diagram for ease of comparison to the other Trees, indicating where the paths have been added or removed.

In this state, our apparent knowledge has risen up to take the position of our crown, replacing divine unity with a state of wilful separation. As *Da'ath* is now triumphant, the path between it and *Kether* is governed here by the Moon, the card illustrating fear, separation, the unconscious, and the illusion of reality. Our highest aspiration and true station has been replaced with a mere shadow, a reflection of our divinity. Through the beauty of correspondence, we see that this path – without the interruption of *Da'ath* – is that of the High Priestess in the "natural" Tree, who corresponds to the Moon. She is the light being reflected by our self-awareness, not by our unconsciousness and base principles.

If we look to the bottom of the Tree, we can also see further illustration of our perilous state. We exist in *Malkuth*, the kingdom and world of action, now under the paths of the Star and the Blasted Tower, with the World before us. We aspire, we hope, we plan and project (Star), yet all comes tumbling down, time and time again (Tower). The World seems a place of some abstract and unseen Judgement – as we see from the position of that card connecting *Yesod* and *Tiphareth*.

Our ego-process in *Yesod* is governed by the Devil and Temperance, the Devil and the Angel on our shoulders, pulling us one way or another, in a constant battle. Our only escape is through the paths of Death and the Hanged Man; transformation and sacrifice, leading to *Tiphareth*.

Once in *Tiphareth*, we have to our two sides the paths of Justice and the Wheel of Fortune; law and luck. We can begin to redeem our arrangement by working with the Hermit and with Strength, attempting to reconcile the dual aspects of our nature through introspection.

In effect, this work, this map, if pursued, leads at this stage of the journey to the initiatory experience of the Neophyte – a breakthrough moment that the world may not be how it appears, that we have some sense of self-direction and responsibility for our own state, and that we must follow that light of our nature. The Tree then becomes better mapped by the "natural" model, which is thus brought into our focus.

To conclude our brief observations on this "night before" model, we can see that the Chariot is under the direct influence of *Da'ath*, which connects it to *Geburah*, severity. This is the worst possible approach to self-control and direction. It is the "life coach" that believes everything they say, whilst their life is a mess, it is the cult leader, or the presentation of a glossy life that only exists on social media by someone who is trying to hold together mental health issues. Or it is at best simply the person who is sure about their life and is getting on with making it a success, with no regard to any other considerations beyond that success.

On the other side of the Tree in this state, we have the Lovers, which connects *Da'ath* to *Chesed*, meaning 'loving kindness'. It is again the worst sort of love – manipulative and directing, self-loathing, co-dependent, a travesty of relationship. The wrong type of self-assurance has elevated *Da'ath* and it eats up all that should come from *Chesed* and flow below.

The Sun is at midnight in this map, sat between *Tiphareth*, to which it corresponds, and its counterpart, *Da'ath*. It is upon a path no longer directly connected to *Kether* as it is in the redeemed model.

All light is swallowed up in knowledge, but this knowledge is born of the state of separation, and it maintains this separation, even as we try and learn that it could be otherwise.

As a black hole, *Da'ath* also swallows *Binah* and *Chockmah*, through the paths now bent to it and illustrated by the Empress and the High Priestess. All nature, all our intuition, even divine inspiration, becomes drawn into our absolute knowledge of our own apparent state. In that moment, all is lost.

To either side of us in this higher level of the Tree are the Hierophant and Emperor, the masculine counterparts to the High Priestess and the Empress. They preside in the worst possible places, with the Emperor bringing the unbounded energy of *Chockmah* into the expansiveness of *Chesed*. This is power for its own sake, expansionist policies and scorched earth scenarios. There are no reins on the power-mad and compassion is perverted to dictatorship. On the side of the Hierophant, he is now placed between *Binah*, the *Sephirah* of structure, and *Geburah*, that of severity. He is the religious regime, the tradition that will suffer no change, persecution and the inquisition.

Finally, in this abhorrent and fallen Tree, the Magician and the Fool keep to their places, as being close to *Kether* they cannot be subverted as easily as the other archetypes. They remain the Spirit and the Will, given to us to escape this broken world and to return the fruit of the Tree to the original garden from whence it was stolen.

Aleister Crowley's Variation to the GD System
In 1904, the magician Aleister Crowley experienced a powerful spiritual encounter with an entity whom he claimed had dictated to him a prophetic text over the course of three days. This text became known as *Liber AL vel Legis*, the *Book of the Law*. Whilst a short piece of text, it is dense and abstract, full of fire and fury, and infused with the high poetry of spiritual vision. It is also replete with riddles and kabbalistic allusions, which were later to form the

backdrop of Crowley's tarot deck designed with Frieda Harris, the *Thoth Tarot*.

Throughout his life, Crowley wrestled with the complexity of this received text, and wrote elaborate commentaries on its many mysteries. There is one particular verse which whilst terse, causes a complication in our correspondence system, as Crowley received this line:

> All these old letters of my Book are aright; but Tzaddi is not the Star. [Liber AI I:57]

Crowley later wrote in his "new" commentary on this line, having only briefly mentioned it in his first commentary:

> Tzaddi is the letter of The Emperor, the Trump IV, and Hé is The Star, the Trump XVII. Aquarius and Aries are therefore counter-changed, revolving on the pivot of Pisces, just as, in the Trumps VIII and XI, Leo and Libra do about Virgo.[25]

He goes on to explain:

> This last revelation makes our Tarot attributions sublimely, perfectly, flawlessly symmetrical. The fact of its so doing is a most convincing proof of the super-human wisdom of the author of this Book to those who have laboured for years, in vain, to elucidate the problems of the Tarot.[26]

However, by the time of his writing of the *Book of Thoth*, first published in 1944, some forty years later, whilst noting that the card of the Emperor is "attributed to the letter Tzaddi",[27] Crowley also appears to correspond the card back to its position on the Tree upon the path of Heh:

---

[25] Crowley, A. *Commentaries*, p. 165
[26] *Ibid*.
[27] Crowley, A. *Book of Thoth*, p. 79

It is finally to be observed that the white light which descends upon him [The Emperor] indicates the position of this card in the Tree of Life. His authority is derived from *Chockmah*, the creative Wisdom, the Word, and is exerted upon *Tiphareth*, the organized man.[28]

He does continue with the Book of the Law switch in his description of the Star card, which is "attributed to the letter Hé, as has been explained elsewhere".[29] In his various other writings, over time, the switch is alluded to where the topic comes up, in various degrees of accessibility.

It is tempting to follow the lead of commentator Lon Milo Duquette on this issue, and utter "Arghhhh!" and "move on - please!".[30] In fact, we shall do so, although not without making a further point for readers, as Crowley himself offers little more to say on the matter.

We might consider that this singular twist of the Emperor and the Star reveals to us either a particular re-mapping of the landscape of life through Crowley's vision – and/or a reflection of the change of Aeon as Crowley presents in the *Book of the Law*. In brief, Crowley suggested that we were at the end of an age of approximately 2,000 years, the Age of Osiris, and moving into a new age, that of Horus. These two ancient Egyptian deities for Crowley carried the significance of the old and new age; the former, a time of patriarchy and religion, the latter a time of individualism and self-determination – he called this *Thelema*, the Greek word for Will.

So the Star, which he expressly equated with the individual Will, and the Emperor, equated with government and paternal power (see *BOT*, p. 77-8), are the ideal images to swap to indicate the replacement of one by another in the passing of one Aeon to another. Whilst they both remain on the Tree, their position in society is altered, as society itself moves to a new paradigm.

---

[28] *Ibid*.
[29] *Ibid*, p. 109
[30] Duquette, L. M. *Understanding Aleister Crowley's Thoth Tarot*, p. 107.

If we are working with *Thelema*, or mapping out our own individual course in this new Aeon, perhaps we might use the map with this switch, and see if it provides more focus on that particular aspect of our journey.

The Waite-Trinick System

A. E. Waite did not leave his tarot work behind after his "delightful experiment" (as he called it) with Pamela Colman-Smith in 1909 when they created what is now the world's most iconic deck. Some ten years later, between 1917-1923, he worked with stained glass artist J. B. Trinick to create a secret set of tarot images for the Major Arcana, to be used in ritual and contemplation within his magical order, the F.R.C. or Fellowship of the Rosy Cross.

In the previously unpublished typescripts describing these cards, Waite gave a clear indication of a variant set of correspondences to that used by the Golden Dawn and later modified only slightly by Crowley. Waite's system was a radical overhaul of the correspondences based on his conception of the *Shekinah* (the presence of God in the world, usually depicted as feminine) and his version of Catholic Mysticism.

In overview, it appears to make as much sense, if not more, than the Golden Dawn model, if we consider a tighter correspondence to the concepts of the Tree of Life. However, as we have already covered, every map has its own utility, and Waite's is specific in mapping to particular concepts in Kabbalah that were not of such peculiar significance to the founders of the Golden Dawn.

Illus. Tarot Cards on Tree of Life (Waite-Trinick System).

We see in Waite's map that the Empress and the Emperor are placed at the top of the Tree, rather than the Fool and the

Magician. In this we might see the fundamental difference of the two maps; Waite's is primarily of mystical intent, the Golden Dawn of magical intent. His version places the divine feminine and masculine potencies enthroned atop the Tree, the GD place the spiritual seeker and the magician at the end of their journey and attaining mastery. It is a fine if not totally insubstantial difference in the end, but for now it will suffice to explore the two models as being different in this regard.

The Waite-Trinick model also continues logically the theme of masculine and feminine in having the High Priestess descend from *Binah* to *Geburah* on the feminine pillar of form, and in balance, the Magician descend from *Chockmah* to *Chesed* on the masculine pillar of force. We see from this suggested a connection between the Empress and her emissary on earth, the Priestess, and the Emperor likewise represented by the Magician. In actually reading tarot, these resonances can inform a reading very powerfully.

There are other elements of beauty in the Waite-Trinick model; the stellar cards of the Sun, Moon and Star now all emit from *Netzach*, the *Sephirah* corresponding to Venus and representing Nature and natural cycles.

At a more abstract level, there is also the perfectly balanced trinity of the Sun, Devil and Lovers in the triad of paths below *Tiphareth*, the central *Sephirah* of the Christ-centre. This trinity is clearly depicted in the Waite-Trinick images as Christ (Sun), Lucifer (Devil) and Eden (Lovers), illustrating the fall from grace and redemption through Christ which leads us into the saviour-centre of *Tiphareth*.

As we work with a new model of correspondences, we sometimes have to unlearn or shake out previous connections, which remain as overlays; like still seeing in your imagination a building that used to be there when now another stands in its place. The Wheel of Fortune in Waite's system takes the highest position of all, between *Kether* and *Da'ath*, indicating it contains the most secret and "highest" of mysteries. It now becomes a cosmic symbol, of all time and space, unity beyond comprehension, the divine in all things, not merely the play of a wheel of fortune and fate in life.

We should also note that Waite included *Da'ath* (meaning 'knowledge') as an entity on his map, as he viewed it as a significant spiritual landmark and perhaps saw more in it than the founders of the Golden Dawn. It was also a concept developed further by Crowley in his writings upon the Abyss and *Da'ath*, and further by Kenneth Grant.

As a result of this incorporation of *Da'ath*, we split two paths into half, each with their own tarot card correspondences, and as a result have to lose two paths. There are many variant models of the Tree of Life, and Waite could have chosen to lose the bottom two diagonal paths, connecting *Hod* and *Netzach* to *Malkuth*, but instead dropped the two diagonal paths connecting *Binah* and *Chockmah* to *Tiphareth*. In this way he removed direct connections from the Upper Triad to *Tiphareth* save through the path of the Fool through *Da'ath*. We will see that the Fool is represented by Waite as a Cosmic Christ, hence making sense of this alternate schema.

In the descriptions below I have also paraphrased, re-presented or interpreted Waite's unpublished writings on the Waite-Trinick Tarot which I am not able to reproduce in their original form or in their entirety.

1. Malkuth
From *Malkuth* reaches the path of *Tau*, illustrated by the World card. This is one of five cards that remain in the same place on the Tree of Life in both the Golden Dawn system and the Waite-Trinick systems, the others being Temperance, Hermit, Devil, and the Hanged Man.

The symbolism is much the same as Waite utilised in his deck with Pamela Colman-Smith, but in his private writings some ten years later he was able to discuss more about his interpretation of the card, about which he had only alluded in his earlier *Pictorial Key to the Tarot* (1910).[31]

Waite saw the image as that of Nature, a woman, but also the divine presence in all things, both within us and without us, the *Shekinah*. We discuss the *Shekinah* further in this present book and it is of utmost importance in Waite's life-work.

She is also the guardian of the gate into the world of formation; as we first step upon the mystical path, we leave the world of our senses and enter the world of our imagination, which formulates all things; we come to see how we create our own version of the World. We learn in the world card, both naked and veiled, how images arise of nature within us, and what might lie before our expression of that mystery. Her various symbols are intended to show the comprehensive model of all we might attain, the unity behind all separate displays of that unity.

Also leading out of *Malkuth* is the path of *Shin*, which in this system corresponds to the Blasted Tower, rather than the Last Judgement, which Waite moved higher up the Tree. This image is definitely equated by the Golden Dawn as the Tower of Babel, and Waite picks up on that meaning of overthrow – in the Golden Dawn image, the two figures thrown out of the Tower were said to be the King who some stories have constructing the Tower, Nimrod and his Vizier.

In at least following the general Order teaching to this point, Waite suggests that the Tower is the pinnacle of the mind, the state of separation (divorce) in which we find ourselves at the beginning of our journey. Our words are not born of the Word and our utterances are in a language of confusion. When we enter the mystical life, we must prepare for our mind to be destroyed by the divine will, as we engage in spiritual work to break up our personality structure.

As a counterpoint to this process - for nothing is unbalanced in the Tree other than ourselves as we make the journey – is the Star card connecting *Malkuth* and *Netzach*.

---

[31] See Goodwin, T. & Katz, M. *Secrets of the Waite-Smith Tarot*.

The Star here fits beautifully the *Sepher Yetzirah* description of the 30th path, which is "the collecting intelligence, so called because Astrologers deduce from it the judgement of the Stars, and of the celestial signs, and the perfections of their science, according to the rules of their revolutions".

The Star is that which collects the broken pieces of the Tower, and the Tower is what we build to reach the Star. Our vision can never be completely realised in this world, so we keep ascending. In a Thelemic sense, the Star represents Will, and here it is our sense of personal will and independence, which will later be turned into a pure channel for divine will once the lesson of the Tower is truly comprehended. As it is written, "Except the LORD build the house, they labour in vain that build it: except the LORD keep the city, the watchman waketh but in vain" [Psalm 127:1].

2. Yesod

In *Yesod* we connect to *Tiphareth* via the image of **Temperance**, which Waite viewed as the will toward re-birth. She is the *Shekinah* that reconciles the confession of sin with the sanctifying grace of God. Her two chalices represent the influence of *Chesed* and *Geburah* passing through *Tiphareth* (the *Shekinah* is also seen as the vessel of the *Messiah*) through *Yesod* and into *Malkuth* through the path of the World. These two great powers are as water and fire; purification and consecration.

The card shows how we must ascend in our sacramental life and attain salvation, as the chalice is symbolic of benediction, the meeting of our prayer for blessing and the bestowal of that blessing.

As a bridge between our world and that of the divine, Waite saw Temperance as the equivalent of the Bronze Laver, the bowl that was placed half-way between the brazen altar and the holy place in the Temple of Solomon. Here Temperance is placed between *Yesod* and *Tiphareth*, thus corresponding to the Temple of Solomon, with *Tiphareth* as the Inner Sanctuary.

In the Waite-Trinick Tarot, the symbolism is further picked up with the placement of a Scallop Shell which is symbolic of baptism and is painted by Trinick as being the commencement of the path between what Waite calls the last mystery of the rose-cross, as the initiate enters into *Tiphareth*.

Also connecting from *Yesod*, to *Netzach*, is the path of the Moon. Waite again sees this as an aspect of the *Shekinah*, at this lower level reflecting the light of the Sun, corresponding to *Tiphareth* and the card of the Sun itself, radiating also out of *Netzach* but to *Tiphareth*. The Moon is our natural mind, caught between the limits of the visible world, the two towers. It is the illusion of thought, when it is not self-aware and transcended. The trap on this path is the glamour and uncertainty of thought itself, when we get caught into trying to make logical sense of all things, even our spiritual life.

Waite maintains common symbolism on the card in the Waite-Trinick image, having the crayfish as representing our evil part, always trying to rise up into our mind from the depths, and the two dogs as our degenerated nature, holding us in bay by its own fear lest we attempt the process of regeneration and redemption.

So we do not progress to *Netzach* from *Yesod*, as our mind must be made self-aware first, else it get caught in its own machinations. It is for good reason that *Yesod* is also referred to as the "treasure-house of images", and a clockwork museum in which many are lost.

From *Yesod* to *Hod* we take the path of Justice, clearly held by Waite to be in two forms; natural justice and divine justice. He sees it as evidence that the mind reflects the higher, for we bring the notion of justice into our life, therefore it must exist as a template in the higher realm. Justice is here leading us from a life of separation to a life of union.

Within the secret rituals of Waite's magical order is a beautiful wording of the tradition, wherein it is described that when we sit in a place of union, we have Hades (Lucifer/Devil) on our left, the Garden of Eternity (Paradise/Lovers) on our right, the Angel of

Death (here Justice with her Sword presiding over the dead souls) above us, and the Tree of Life behind us. This is a statement of our position on the Tree of Life in this specific grade, according to these correspondences and their layout and positions on the Tree. It is a demonstration of how these maps are used within ritual to initiate complex appreciation of deep patterns in nature and the divine.

As it might be said with regard to ritual, if you receive these messages truly within your heart, you will be travelled to those places in spirit.

3. Hod
As we will see in *Netzach*, certain paths are blocked to our progress as we ascend the Tree of Life. The path of *Samekh*, to which corresponds the Devil, is sealed to us, as we have to yet progress to *Netzach* from *Hod*; we cannot take a short-cut to *Tiphareth*. In fact, we will find ourselves turned back from *Netzach* too, only to have to return to the middle path and enter *Tiphareth* through the path of Temperance.

The warning about short-cuts is implicit in the card image being that of Lucifer; as we trace what Waite calls the path of liberation, we are tempted by the desire for spirituality, and spiritual things. We might come to believe we are on a path of attainment, rather than surrender, and in doing so fall into bondage of the most evil kind; to that of our own separation and agency.

Hod also connects to *Netzach* through the Lovers card, although this would have been shown earlier in the journey to the initiate at the stage of *Yesod*, as the path stretches across their view from that point, looking up the middle pillar. The Lovers is a symbol of the mystic marriage, that of the feminine aspect of the divine, the *Shekinah* and the male aspect of the divine, the *Messiah*. It is a second birth of spiritual consciousness, a regeneration of our soul as we draw together all the parts of our personality for redemption.

Above *Hod* is the Hanged Man, the closed path to *Geburah* and one of the most variant of images in Waite's work (and in some versions of the Golden Dawn) in its symbolism. Whilst often depicted as a literal hanging man, the image can also be a drowned or sleeping giant; the symbolism of the divine hidden within all manifest nature. This is barely intimated by the halo in the Waite-Smith Tarot, and Waite plays his most coy in *Pictorial Key* with his notes that it "is a card of profound significance, but all the signification is veiled", and that in other (false) interpretations, "we may exhaust all published interpretations and find only vanity".[32]

We encounter this sleeping figure later in the journey on the path of *Teth*, the Last Judgement, where he is awakened within us and seen to be the Divine in the Universe and our very soul, but here he is asleep, the signal drowned in noise.

Waite writes of this image as "immanency" which is a fundamental concept in Kabbalah, in addition to the concepts of emanation and to some extent, exemplarism. The divine is not seen as some distant entity but present in all things in different graduation, so all things are examples of the divine. This is seen in the lessons of each path as we progress up the Tree; that each teaches us of the nature of the divine in the unknowable *Sephiroth*, so we can learn and align those lessons to our life, ultimately removing the illusionary separation between ourselves and the divine.

This is the outward expression of the inner realisation of *Tiphareth*, so we do not yet comprehend it and pass from *Hod* to *Netzach*. It is only later that we look from *Geburah*, the House of Death and see the true nature of this Resurrection; that when we die spiritually, we become empty to the divine, and only the divine can fulfil us. This realisation of the Hanged Man is what takes us across the path of the Last Judgement.

4. Netzach
During the work of this grade in the journey of re-birth, Waite considers that we govern ourselves under the rule of "purified will". As he also sees Christ as representing the prototypical adept within

---

[32] Waite, A. E. *Pictorial Key to the Tarot*, p. 116.

the initiate, this will is one which is aligned to our role as mediator of the divine. Out of *Netzach* to *Tiphareth* stretches the path of *Nun*, to which the Sun card corresponds, but we are not able to enter *Tiphareth* along this way, says Waite, following the Golden Dawn ritual initiation sequence.

We must remember that our map here is of a dynamic journey of ascent, rather than an open series of paths and landmarks. It is like climbing a mountain, we often find a route blocked to us until we return in better conditions, or with better tools, or more experience. Sometimes we have to find a detour as the most direct route is impassable. Sometimes we have to check alternative routes before making our ascent up the route originally planned. Initiation is not a direct and open path.

So the image here that Waite uses for the Sun, of Christ with hands extended in healing, emblazoned with the Sun, is showing the promise of Adepthood, a re-investment of one's place in the eternal "beauty" of *Tiphareth*.

The paths, and hence the Major Arcana, to Waite, are the images of sanctification; a close union with God and resultant moral perfection. In this he follows the tarot tradition of virtues; each card being an increasingly higher virtue in a particular sequence.

5. Tiphareth
We will examine the symbolism of the Hermit card in the *Sephirah* of *Chesed*, even though it leaves from *Tiphareth*, as it will be easier to highlight particular aspects of the card in the light of *Chesed*.

Tiphareth, as we noted in the introduction of this section, resides upon the triad of Lucifer (Devil), Christ (Sun) and the Garden of Eden (Lovers) with the Angel of Reconciliation pouring forth from it the four rivers of Eden to Malkuth, where they are received as baptism for the return journey.

Further, Death, the Hermit and the Fool are illustrated on the paths leading out of *Tiphareth* up the Tree, with the Last Judgement card on the path running above the *Sephirah*.

It is certainly the mystical death that is enshrined in the Waite-Trinick image of the Death card. Whilst we live the life of adepthood in *Tiphareth*, reborn in a new form of consciousness, in *Geburah* we must learn to die and leave buried that old sense of selfhood, for a new life in *Chesed*, exempt from all former estates.

Waite speaks of the parallels in all forms of symbolism; that actual death and mystical death have correspondences, and everything in deep spiritual life has its equivalent in life as it is manifest in the everyday world. In *Geburah* come to exist in a state between life and death, it is a dispassionate equilibrium which is almost a constant trance, yet one of awakening. It is this state that is then exhausted and collapsed upon the Last Judgement path when we enter into *Chesed*. It is suggested by Waite in this precise mapping that there is no way to this union unless we pass through the mystical death, and find our resurrection – through the path of Last Judgement.

6. Geburah

The most salient symbol of *Geburah* is that given to the path of *Teth* which connects it across to *Chesed*, and here corresponding to the Last Judgement card. Waite connects this card with the Hanged Man, or submerged divinity, which descends from *Geburah* to *Hod*. The rainbow symbolism is seen in both, as they are both bridges and covenants seen from the place of Death. The other such bridge and covenant is the High Priestess, whose path we do not tread but leads up to *Binah*.

If we look down, we see only the unknown depths and sense dimly our own sleeping spirit. If we look across, to where we must go next, we see the realisation of adepthood, the resurrection of that spirit in the radiance of the divine. Waite calls this the solstice of the eternal summer, and the restoration of the world through the awakening of the highest of lights. It is the grade of the *Adeptus*

Exemptus in *Chesed* to which our attention is taken with the Last Judgement card leading from *Geburah*.

Geburah indeed is the House of Death and where we must overcome concupiscence, in all its forms as the strong life-force that denies death and resists that ultimate transfiguration.

The High Priestess connects *Geburah* to *Binah*, the place of the supernal Eden, of which *Malkuth* is a reflection, and is seen by Waite as the process of absorption. She is the *Shekinah* in the form of the archetypal soul, in whose image our very soul is created – she is thus the Mother of All Souls. Her Work is that of Love, or Union, shown by every path we have journeyed, and leading ultimately to one destination; the Crown of *Kether*. In that love we are utterly absorbed after all trial and judgement, after all restitution. All this happens in *Binah*, the uttermost and all-consuming *Sephirah* of final Understanding.

Waite and Trinick depicted their High Priestess as a heavenly figure being drawn down into the body of a worshipping figure below; or perhaps the figure is arising in spirit into the High Priestess above. The components of *Malkuth* and *Tiphareth*, previously "married" below, are now married again in a spiritualised union which immolates the soul into non-being with God.

7. Chesed
Whilst the Hermit card is first seen from *Tiphareth*, it is here in *Chesed* (to which the path also connects) that its symbolism is most refined. The Hermit is the Keeper of the Secret Tradition, and the light of the divine Word. The light shines through a lantern to symbolise that even at this stage of our ascent, the mysteries are still partially veiled, clouded in language and pretence of understanding. In the mythic story told by Waite, the figure is the messenger of the King's Secrets, the bearer of the secret tradition from *Da'ath* to the three *Sephiroth* of *Chesed*, *Geburah* and *Tiphareth*. In this sense he is the power of the fourth Order, which comprises the highest and most sublime of the initiates who work alone in the World of Ascension.

In our everyday terms, the Hermit is language, symbols, and the way in which our awareness (*Tiphareth*) receives and formulates the most abstract and rarefied of impressions (*Chesed*) during our engagement with reality.

Similarly, the Hierophant illustrates the path connecting *Chesed* back down to *Netzach*. This is not a path that is travelled in the journey up the Tree, as Waite says of his system that it is only concerned with the channels of grace, and following those back to union. The path of the Hierophant is one third of a triad with the Hermit (the Word) and the Sun (Christ), and represents the Official Church. As such, it is all churches and regulation of the Word of God through Christ whereas the Hanged Man on the opposite side of the Tree is the hidden tradition of self-realisation.

Waite also equates each path with its text in the *Sepher Yetzirah*, which he consistently refers to as "the hidden tradition". It is this "hidden tradition" that he makes reference to several times in *Pictorial Key to the Tarot* and is the key to unlocking how he saw the mysteries of the Minors – by referencing them to the *Sepher Yetzirah*.

In every case as we progress in our journey, we must make the symbols alive in us, through not only contemplation but activity; we must align our life to their teaching and integrate their philosophy into our actions and decisions, not merely reduce them into our own choices and predilections.

Da'ath
Waite saw *Da'ath* as of paramount importance in his spiritual map, the most significant landmark of mystical experience. He terms it variously the Secret Palace, the Everlasting Hill of Vision, the Hidden Church, the Holy of Holies, and views it as the attainable threshold of all which is divine.

In the Waite-Trinick images is an illustration corresponding to *Da'ath*, in the manner of the tarot images, so much so that at first we were led to believe it was an image of the Hierophant or perhaps the Emperor, even the Ace of Cups. It shows a Priest in the Order of Melchizedeck, offering the sacrament of wafer and wine in a chalice. In the background stands a city or church, which is the Higher Salem, wherein are the beloved congregation.[33]

Its mystical experience is of the highest order, the union of subject and object in a point of everlasting spiritual ecstasy. It is endless peace and the perfect realisation of all seeking. In the esoteric system called the Astrology of the Soul, *Da'ath* corresponds to Saturn, a dark and secret light.

Like a cosmological black hole, *Da'ath* draws in and out the light, clothing it with manifest symbols and withdrawing those symbols on the event horizon of our souls return.

Below *Da'ath* is the Fool, which for Waite is the macrocosmic Christ, a figure drawn by Trinick as a naked (and apparently asexual) Christ with stigmata, suspended under the huge black sphere of *Da'ath*. This is the anti-self, the negation of the self-centre of *Tiphareth*. The Adept looks up from their position in *Tiphareth* and sees nothing, for there is nothing there that the self can recognise, as no Self is present in that Higher Realm. Thus the initiate continues instead on their journey to *Geburah* through the Death card, dying a slow spiritual death when the most immediate step (off the cliff leaving the Dog of Faith behind) was in front of them all the time. A Fool's Journey indeed.

Above *Da'ath* is the Wheel, connecting to *Kether*, the Crown and *Sephirah* numbered One on the Tree of Life. If we were to make a sentence of these two words, it would be "Knowledge of the Crown", in effect, the knowledge of God. So Waite's Wheel is somewhat more than the fickle acting out of fate and fortune in our world; it is the transcendent glory and joy of union with God. In this manner, the path is described in the *Sepher Yetzirah*, as "the uniting intelligence" and is so called because "it is itself the essence of Glory. It is the consummation of the Truth of individual spiritual

---

[33] Goodwin, T. & Katz, M. *Abiding in the Sanctuary*, pp. 88-9.

things". In the Waite-Trinick image, the Wheel is held in the breast of the *Shekinah*, presenting the knowledge of divinity in the centre of the axle of all creation.

We come here at last to see that light which shone in the darkness, and we comprehend it.[34]

8. Binah

We have described the High Priestess previously, and will describe the Empress when we come to look at *Kether* below; the remaining path connecting to *Binah* is that of Strength. This illustrates the connection between *Binah* ('understanding') and *Da'ath* ('knowledge') so we see in the Waite-Trinick images a very different symbolism to that of a Lion and a Maiden.

Strength is depicted by Trinick as a feminine angel whose hair falls behind her almost to her ankles, polarising both cultivated and wild energies in one image. She is that which holds as the Chariot is that which releases. She is the Being to his Going.

When we consider that *Binah* is the *Sephirah* of structure, atop the pillar of Form, and provides the matrix for all creation, and *Da'ath* is a non-*Sephirah*, something that arises between *Chockmah* and *Binah* as a necessity of their engagement, we might see that there is a tension between these emanations. It is akin to that of a heavy superstar orbiting a black hole – vast interplays of incomprehensible forces and gravitational stresses, bending not only light, but time.

Strength is the illustration of this silent dance of intolerable stress; not only at a cosmic and metaphysical layer, but in the very atoms and quantum forces operating in your own body, and every pattern of your life.

---

[34] For an overview of the concept of negativity in Christian mysticism, see Turner, D. *The Darkness of God*.

9. Chockmah

We will consider the Emperor in our text on *Kether* below, and look at the Chariot and the Magician that connect *Chockmah* to *Da'ath* and *Kether* respectively. The Chariot to Waite is symbolic of the Prince of the Elect, a chosen one who has attained the highest knowledge. Yet, as he briefly teases in the *Pictorial Key to the Tarot*, he is one who would not be able to answer to the High Priestess. This is a candid yet concealed statement to the effect that the mind and learnt knowledge (*Da'ath*) will take you so far in your chariot, but only by grace and through experience (High Priestess) can the final stages be undertaken in the Work.

The Magician likewise is placed between *Chockmah* and *Chesed* to signify that he too may have mastered all the elements, but he must leave these toys behind to attain Wisdom (*Chockmah*) and become the Emperor to sit beside the throne of God (*Kether*).

10. Kether

Into *Kether* we return through the final symbols of the Great Paths; we have seen the Wheel above *Da'ath*, and from the pillars on each side of the temple are the paths of the Empress and the Emperor, the potencies of form and force, of structure and energy, of feminine and masculine. They are the final dualities that are resolved in the unity of *Kether*; all duality and all division.

At this level it is more difficult to consider these images as separate or individual; all the symbols becoming more closely united as we reach up the Tree of Life. In the World card below, we saw each symbol laid out and separate; now we return to the world in which all symbols are obsolete.

The Empress is enthroned upon the oceans of night in *Binah*, and the Emperor presides over the quarry of devotion, *Chockmah*. They are the realisation of divine understanding and wisdom in the world. They are transitory in their rulership and aegis as are all things, yet remain as abiding patterns, revolving forever upon the wheel of creation.

We can also see these as the three great forces of the universe in all triune forms; the creator in the Empress, the destroyer in the Emperor and the Maintainer in the Wheel.

Having looked specifically at these versions of the whole map, and how it can be utilised to model, locate and predict our experience of the territory of magical and spiritual experience, we will now return to the history and development of the Kabbalah, and then look at each *Sephirah* in detail.

The Tree of Sapphires

Voices of the Word, Leaves of the Light

As we have touched upon, the Kabbalah (a Hebrew word meaning "handed down" or "oral tradition") is the term used to denote a general set of esoteric or mystical teachings originally held within Judaism, but later promulgated to a wider audience in the 12th century onwards through centres of learning such as Toledo in Spain. It consists of a body of teachings and analysis dealing with the nature of the Universe, aspects of divinity, and the method of creation. From this set of teachings is derived the role of man in the revealed scheme of things.

The history of the Kabbalah is difficult to fix to dates and linear sequences of succession due to its nature as oral, traditional, teachings. Long before printing presses, the Kabbalistic teachings were passed from teacher to pupil as oral teachings and collections of manuscripts, which in turn may have been copies of other sets being used by other teachers. The original impulse of Kabbalah, however, emerged from a first century school of Jewish mysticism termed *Merkabah*, meaning 'chariot'. These mystics utilised secret methods of spiritual ascent in order to attain mystical experience.[35] These experiences can be recognised as those common to any modern adept following the occult initiatory system, for example; "the world changed into purity around me, and my heart felt as if I had entered a new world".[36]

The teachings of the *Merkabah* mystics became part of the *Heikhalot* school, whose name means 'palace', referring to the spiritual planes through which the mystics ascended. The description of these journeys seems to bear similarities to the journey of the soul into the Underworld depicted in the ancient Egyptian *Book of Coming Forth by Day*, with magical words or

---

[35] An interesting title aiming to recover the shamanic nature of Judaic ritual practice is Winkler, G. *Magic of the Ordinary.*
[36] *Merkabah Shelemah* 1a, 4b. in Scholem, G. *Kabbalah*, p. 18.

appropriate names of the gods to be spoken before each door is passed and each palace entered.

Three classical texts formulate the basic structure of traditional Kabbalah, being:

> The Sefer-ha-Zohar; Book of Splendour - First printed 1558-60 and 1559-60
>
> The Sefer Yetzirah; Book of Formation - First printed in Mantua 1562
>
> The Sefer-ha-Bahir; Book of Light - First printed in Amsterdam 1651

The collective writings that became the *Holy Zohar* are now widely acknowledged to be the work of Moses de León, dating from 1280. These dense and complex writings, written in Aramaic, emerged in Spain and rapidly become a foundation stone of Kabbalistic study.

Many of the later Kabbalistic schools are formed about these books, finding in them interpretation and meanings revealing the work of God and Creation. The school formed at Safed in the sixteenth century produced many of the leading thinkers of Kabbalah, particularly Rabbi Isaac Luria, called the Ari (1534-1572), and Rabbi Moshe Cordevero, the Ramak (1522-1570). The former is responsible for much of the current structure and cosmology of Kabbalah, as the Lurianic school of thought provided answers to many of the more complex issues of Kabbalistic thought, particularly relating to the 'breaking of the vessels'.

The next major historical development of Kabbalah came with the formation of the Hasidic Movement in the mid 1700's, based around the Rabbi Israel, more commonly known as the Baal Shem Tov (1698-1760), which means 'master of the word', a high mark of respect in Kabbalism.

Having briefly examined the development of Kabbalah within the Judaic mystical tradition, we must now attempt to sketch some of the significant points at which it passed through to the occult tradition, particularly in Europe, and then to the modern Magician.

The Kabbalah and its teachings passed across into the magical philosophy primarily by transition through medieval Christian thinkers who saw in Kabbalah a model and validation for their own tradition. From the late fifteenth century Jewish converts to Christianity brought Kabbalistic views to the attention of other theologians. A Platonic Academy in Florence, founded by Giovanni Mirandola (1463-94) furthered research and discussion of Kabbalah amongst the philosophers of the time. The later publication of the *Shaarey Orah*, 'Gates of Light' in Latin (1516) brought further interest in the teachings of the *Bahir* and the fundamental plan of the Tree of Life.

The prime source for the precursors of the occult revival were without question Athanasius Kircher (1602-80), a German Jesuit whose *Oedipus Aegyptiacus* (1652) detailed Kabbalah amongst its study of Egyptian mysteries and hieroglyphics, and Cornelius Agrippa's *De Occulta Philosophia* (1533).

Other works, such as those from alchemists including Khunrath, Fludd and Vaughan indicated that the Kabbalah had become the convenient meta-map for early hermetic thinkers. Christian mystics began to utilise its structure for an explanation of their revelations, the most notable being Jacob Boeheme (1575-1624). However, the most notable event in terms of our line of examination is the publication of Christian Knorr Von Rosenroth's (1636-89) *Kabbala Denudata* in Latin in 1677 and 1684, which provided translations from the *Zohar* and extracts from the works of Issac Luria.

It was this work which, when translated into English by MacGregor Mathers (1854-1918) in 1887 as *The Kabbalah Unveiled*, alongside already existing translations of the *Sepher Yetzirah*, provided the Kabbalistic backbone of the Golden Dawn Society, from which issued many of the more recent occult Kabbalists, such as Dion Fortune (1891-1946), who summarised the *Sephiroth* in her *Mystical Qabalah* (1935) and Aleister Crowley (1898-1947). The

Christian occultist and Golden Dawn member, A. E. Waite also produced many works examining the secret tradition of Kabbalah, although of all of these occultists, Gershom Scholem says that they relied more on their imagination rather than their knowledge of Kabbalah, which he saw as "infinitesimal".[37]

Another stream stemming from Rosenroth's work came through Eliphas Levi (1810-75), who became familiar with Cabalistic Martinism through Hoene Wronski (1778-1853), and had read both Boehme and Rosenroth amongst many others. He also became a student of tarot through the writings of Court de Gebelin (1725-84), who ascribed to the tarot an ancient Egyptian origin. From de Gébelin and Rosenroth, Levi synthesised a scheme of attribution of the tarot cards to the twenty-two paths of the Tree of Life, a significant development in that it provided a synthetic model of processes to be later modified and used by the Golden Dawn as mapping the initiation system of psychological, occult, and spiritual development. Levi wrote, "Qabalah ... might be called the mathematics of human thought".[38] Aleister Crowley continued Levi's work to some extent in his seminal work on the tarot, *The Book of Thoth*, published originally in the *Equinox* III.5, 1944.

In summary, the Kabbalah passed from Judaic tradition through to Christian tradition, and through other flowerings such as the Polish Jewry Kabbalistic revival in the eighteenth century. Many of the early hermetic scholars and Neoplatonic thinkers began to merge Kabbalah with other doctrines such as Alchemy, and later occultists utilised it as a grand plan of spiritual ascent, bringing it full circle to its origins in the chariot riding of the mystics from which the tradition stemmed.

It is said by traditional Kabbalists and Kabbalistic scholars that the occultist has an imperfect knowledge of the Tree, and hence the work of such is corrupt. I would argue that the Kabbalah is a basic device whose keys are infinite and that any serious approach to its

---

[37] Scholem, G. *Kabbalah*, p. 203.
[38] Levi, E. *The Book of Splendours*, p. 127.

basic meta-system will reveal some relevance if tested in the world about us, no matter how it may be phrased. The first Kabbalists cannot be said to have had an imperfect knowledge because they did not understand or utilize information systems theory or understand modern cosmology. Indeed, their examination of themselves and the Universe revealed resonant thinking many hundreds of years before science formalized it, in the same way that some current esoteric thinking may be reframed in some new science a hundred or a thousand years in the future.

The body of teaching has various traditions and groupings of belief, but most hold as their central model a diagram generally composed of ten circles joined by twenty-two lines, entitled the *Otz Ch'im* or 'Tree of Life'. These circles represent the ten concepts called *Sephiroth*, a Hebrew word meaning 'numerical emanations', and are said to represent every aspect of existence. The lines connecting them are termed 'paths' and are taken to represent the nature of the twenty-two letters of the Hebrew alphabet, which (unlike English and similar languages) are also concepts and numbers equally as we have seen. The *Sephiroth* are also seen as paths, and so the full Tree has thirty-two paths.

To this basic diagram have been attributed various other systems and attributions of elements from other systems. Therefore, the twenty-two Major Arcana of the tarot cards have been linked (in various formats) to the paths, and the planets, elements, stages of alchemy and other aspects of esoteric teachings have been linked to the *Sephiroth*. The majority of these attributions are derivations and permutations of those developed by medieval Hermeticists, who painstakingly produced tables of every angelic hierarchy, every grade of demon, and even the occult connections between rocks and stars. The *Magus; Celestial Intelligencer* (1801) of Francis Barrett is an example of these tables of correspondence and the occult dictionary *777* by Crowley provides a synopsis of the major systems of magical correspondence (i.e. deities, zodiacal signs, planets, perfumes, colours, numbers, mythical animals etc.). The basic elements of correspondence are shown in table two. These tables were also to be found as early as 1533 in Book II of Agrippa's *Occult Philosophy*, as mentioned earlier.

Rather than examining any of these many elements in detail, we will sketch a number of basic concepts that apply throughout any examination of the multiple facets of this meta-system, specifically where recent advances in information technology and related systems have provided new conceptual models and terms for utilising this highly advanced esoteric and mystical framework.

One of the prime tenets of occult belief is the law of correspondence, or "like affects like". This states that due to the inherent unity of all things, certain items and concepts have a type of mutual sympathy, association, or relationship. A primal application of this law is seen in the action of the witchdoctor or sorcerer who gains an item belonging to that of the individual he wishes to influence, be it for healing or cursing, or with or without the individual's knowledge. Other more esoteric correspondences are seen across sets of items, for example, numbers, planets, scents and colours. An example is that the colour green, the number seven and the emotion of love are associated with each and the planet Venus, also viewed as the Greek Goddess of Love. A Magician attempting to invoke the influence of this Goddess is likely to surround himself with items which resonate with her.

This occult idea has a psychological parallel in colour theory, which has demonstrated that certain colours produce changes in our internal physical and psychological states. A biological theory of morphic resonance has recently been postulated as detailing a non-local field which determines the manifestation of living things, and this relies on a similar basic view of occult inter-connectivity. Although many traditional Kabbalists abhor magical systems of correspondence, it is evident that early Kabbalists utilized this law in apportioning letters of the Hebrew alphabet to certain aspects of God. In a sense, the same unity of things is being demonstrated across sets of objects by the process of digitization becoming frequent in media communications. Thus, a sound can be reduced to a representation of zeros and ones and signalled in any other set of items, such as colour, shapes or even tactile signals. In the future, it may well be possible to transmit Beethoven's Fifth Symphony directly as colours and sensations to a data-suit which the receiver wears and through which the senses are stimulated.

The Tree as a Meta-model (Template Theory)

In many Kabbalistic aphorisms, the basic concepts often refer to the Tree of Life as a meta-model, that is, a system capable of comprehending other systems within itself. This is implied when authors use such terms as "universal language", "cosmic plan" and "blue-print of manifestation".

Other esoteric examples of meta-models include the Seven Rays system, the Chakra system, Astrology, and tarot. Earlier meta-models include the Platonic and Pythagorean systems, and the quest for the supreme meta-model continues with the mathematical/physics search for a grand unified field theory (a single theory which relates all other theories regarding cosmological sciences).

The concept of meta-models can be viewed as a template, or perhaps (when utilized in practice) as a filter, through which the infinite and eternal is limited within our own comprehension.

The Tree of Life acts as a template capable of the following functions, listed according to Aleister Crowley and with brief commentary by myself:

(a) *A language fitted to describe certain classes of phenomena, and express certain classes of ideas.*

The eclectic approach of magick and the transcendent experiences of mysticism demand a means of expression not found in language fixed in the apparent world about us. Kabbalah, in providing a system which is both abstract and structural, can be used to provide a common ground of meaning in conceptual realms where even meaning is relative. An example might be found in the way

Kabbalah depicts the interaction of different worlds in the Jacob's Ladder diagram. This basic image can be applied to many phenomena, from the way chemical changes take place when atoms change their energy states, to the way certain beliefs follow different levels of mystical experience. The Kabbalah provides in the first place a language by which mystical ideas can be described and expressed clearly and precisely.

(b) *A terminology by means of which it is possible to equate the mental processes of people apparently diverse.*

One of the key functions of the Tree, and one at which it excels, is as a mental filing-system. Not only can the Tree be viewed as a system, but also a meta-system, that is, a system which includes other systems within it. In this way, ideas may be compared across apparently different models. An example of this is the association of astrological concepts and symbolism with the myths of Ancient Egypt. When we understand the nature of Venus in astrological symbolism, we are able to equate this knowledge with an understanding of the nature of Hathor in Ancient Egyptian cosmology, through their mutual correspondence on the Tree. There are some dangers in taking this approach too simplistically or too far, as there are dangers in all methods of translation and learning. However, the Kabbalah nonetheless provides an incomparable method of accessing a range of new information and rapidly assimilating unfamiliar and diverse systems.

(c) *A system of symbolism which enables thinkers to formulate their ideas with complete precision, and to find simple expression for complex thoughts.*

As a system, Kabbalah offers a simple basis from which can be modelled complex processes. In the science of complexity and fluid dynamic theory, this is termed 'surface complexity arising out of deep simplicity'. As an example, a basic knowledge of the Hebrew letters can be utilized to model any number of dynamic processes taking place in the Universe, through the Hebrew God-names. It provides a map which can model and predict with precision the unfolding of events and states of mind.

(d) *An instrument for interpreting symbols whose meaning has become obscure, forgotten or misunderstood, by establishing a necessary connection between the essence of forms, sounds, simple ideas (such as number) and their spiritual, moral or intellectual equivalents.*

The network structure of the Tree operates as a kind of Akashic Record, a term sometimes used to describe an astral library, accessible through altered states of consciousness such as meditation, dreams, and channelling. The Tree has a holographic structure which ensures that any item of discrete information placed on it will immediately become highlighted by the information already in place throughout the Tree. In this way, the Tree becomes a jigsaw into which pieces have particular, unique positions.

Sometimes a piece may be placed or an idea considered incorrectly, and it is not noticed until you come to fill the pieces in around it. Thus, for some time, one might attribute water to *Yesod*, and come to no real harm or confusion, until one day an increased knowledge of *Hod*, *Netzach* and the Middle Pillar make it apparent not only that the correct and fitting attribution in terms of the system is Air, but why that is the case.

This aspect of Kabbalah also allows us to comprehend obscure symbolism such as alchemy, Enochian, or other systems, by placing them upon the Tree and making maps through correspondence. The Tree in this case becomes a Rosetta Stone allowing us to re-create an entire language through mere fragments of correspondence.

(e) *A system of classification of omniform ideas so as to enable the mind to increase its vocabulary of thoughts and facts through organizing and correlating them.*

It is a commonly accepted fact that memory can be improved by collecting items of information in sets, and the Tree enables one to do this in a similar fashion to the Magic Room memory trick, where a room is strongly visualised in the imagination, and when a list is to be remembered, the items in the list are mentally placed in the room, and so associated with anchors already held in memory. The unlikely juxtapositions so created (a chicken on the shopping list placed in the armchair, and a lettuce inside the goldfish bowl) assist the recall of the list.

Once the basics of the Tree have been mastered, new ideas from any source can be assimilated quickly or at least stored in relevant areas in the structure. The Kabbalistic exercise of Permutations, where letters of a divine name are re-arranged and shuffled in a constant motion during meditation can provide a basis of further exercises where areas of the Tree or tarot Cards are shuffled to provide vast ranges of new insight.

This process has been made more accessible to non-meditators by computer programs such as the original *Brainstorm* or *TurboThought*, which allow the ranking, chaining and shuffling of ideas on a computer screen.

(f) *An instrument for proceeding from the known to the unknown on similar principles to those of mathematics.*

The process of Initiation takes us up through the *Sephiroth* via the Paths and from the apparent world around us into the hidden world of the divine. As the Kabbalistic system is based in simple objects such as the Hebrew letters, which can be arranged in complex formulae or words, which in turn have meaning, we can build up a coherent model of the Universe by simply applying our basic knowledge of the Tree to an event, observing the process, then expanding our model on that basis.

The Tree also manages to recognise the mathematical limit known as Gödel's Incompleteness Theorem, which states that every equation must hold at least one reference that can only be proven outside of that equation, in another equation; therefore, there cannot be a complete or self-contained equation. The outsider equation in the Tree is the *Ain Soph Aur*, (the "limitless light" from which the Tree proceeds) or, in the Paths, the Fool card, which is correctly unnumbered in most packs and therefore outside the scheme.

As we build up our knowledge of the Tree and apply it to our experience through ritual, correspondence and contemplation, it becomes an increasingly elegant and precise model, which allows us to make sense of what otherwise, might be unrecognised or resisted by our limited worldview.

(g) *A system of criteria by which the truth of correspondences may be tested with a view to criticising new discoveries in the light of their coherence with the whole body of truth.*[39]

The testing aspect of the Tree is revealed increasingly as the individual formulates their own cosmology and philosophy in its terms. Analysing correspondences reveals, as does all Inner Work, other levels of meaning, and these can be in turn tested back against the whole pattern of the Tree. The holographic nature of the Tree ensures that each idea or belief that is tested against the Tree is set against the whole system and not merely one aspect of it.

This final aspect of Kabbalah is important in spiritual progress and initiatory work as it allows us to keep a reasonably coherent structure as at the same time we destroy all that structure. It provides a scaffold that we can climb and test its ability to bear us up, even as we remove it behind us. At the end of the *Mutus Liber* alchemical series of drawings, the ladder is drawn up in the final stage.

---

[39] Crowley, *777*, pp. 125-6

The Tree as a Fractal System (The Orchard)

Certain mathematical formulae involving complex numbers composed of both real numbers and imaginary numbers (such as *i*, the symbol denoting the square root of -1) can produce graphs such as the Mandelbrot set which have recursive properties, that is, they repeat their patterns at lower or higher orders of complexity and calculation. Thus, when magnifying, mathematically, an area of the Mandelbrot set, one can find the same strange shape emerging, and within certain areas of that shape, the shape repeats, and so forth. As is said of that and could be said of the Tree of Life and correspondences, "Self-similarity is symmetry across scale".[40]

This discovery reminds us of the Kabbalistic doctrine of *Sephiroth* existing within *Sephiroth*. Indeed, Joseph ibn Sayyah went as far as to describe in detail the play of lights within the *Sephiroth* to the fourth degree, as, for example, the "*Tiferet* which is in *Gedullah* which is in *Binah* which is in *Keter*".

Again, this finds a similarity with one eastern concept which states that there is no beginning, no ending, no linear progression, only an unbounded net of jewels each of which reflects and contains the reflection of each of the others.

Thus, the repetitive plan which is spoken of in Kabbalah, and the fact that each *Sephirah* "contains the other nine", is due to the fractal or recursive nature of the Kabbalistic system symbolised by the Tree of Life, and referred to often as the Orchard of trees.

Another technological advance which resumes this idea is that of hologram images, which are produced by projecting the interference patterns made by light waves (lasers) about an object onto photographic plate. Shining light on the plate from the same angle then produces the image of the object from the viewers location. As Itzhak Bentov explains, if one were to freeze such an interference pattern, for example, the ripples in water made by a stone being dropped, then one could, analysing the pattern,

---

[40] Gleick, J. *Chaos*, p. 103.

discover where the stone had broken through the water.[41] On a note of poetic whimsy, one could perhaps visualise the Tree of Life as the wave-front of the light of God.

One may realise that all the above modern ideas are actually pre-empted and summarised in a more ancient doctrine, which proposes, in the *Tabula Smaragdina* (Table of Emerald); "It is true without lying, certain and most true, that which is inferior or below, is as that which is superior, or above, and that which is superior as that which is inferior, to work and accomplish the miracles of one thing."

Patterns emerge at all levels and all scales, such as the spiral of a shell and the spiral of a fern branch, or the shape of a galaxy and the shape of a human cell. As Louise B. Young states, "the whole is imminent in all the parts, no matter how small".[42] To those who work with such a self-reflexive system, then it becomes possible to model, and experience, states that often defy description in other, more linear systems. As Blake puts it in *Auguries of Innocence*:

> To see a World in a grain of sand,
>
> And a heaven in a wild flower,
>
> Hold infinity in the palm of your hand,
>
> And eternity in an hour.[43]

Such is the promise that the Tree of Sapphires (another translation of the word *Sephirah*) holds, as each facet of each sapphire reflects eternally upon each other in a labyrinth of light.

The Tree as an Emanative System (The Fountain of Light)

One of the earliest exponents of an emanative system was the Neoplatonist Plotinus (c.205-70 AD), for whom Reality could be

---

[41] Bentov, I. *Stalking the Wild Pendulum*, p. 14.

[42] Young, L. B. *The Unfinished Universe*, p. 206.

[43] http://www.poetryfoundation.org/poem/172906 [last accessed 17th June 2015]

visualised as a set of increasingly fragmented reflections, proceeding from the One (or "the Good") to Mind, then to Soul, and then a fading out into blank matter. His philosophy, as compiled in the *Enneads* also contains a doctrine that uses a tri-partate division of the Worlds, as within Kabbalah, and mentioned by some Kabbalistic authors as the Supernal, Moral and Physical Triangles. Mathers termed these the Intellectual, Moral and Material Worlds, but Dion Fortune disagreed with his "misleading translations" and rephrased them as the Supernal, Ethical and Astral Triangles.[44]

Emanative systems are based on the concept of a genesis point which emits a series of hypostases or worlds, which are usually arranged in liner or circular patterns, or some combination, as in the Tree of Life, and then subdivided into hierarchies or orders of being.

Following from this core idea, the human being is then seen as a fragmented reflection of this Source, to which it can attain by contemplation and transcendence of the less real. As Plotinus and Aristotle both perceived it, this contemplation of its own virtue formed a self-similar image which could then, albeit being imperfect, draw vitality from the real and generate more accurate reflections of that Source.

As Plato wrote in *Timaeus* (37 c-d):

> When the father who had engendered it [the universe] saw it in motion and alive, a shrine brought into being for the everlasting gods, he rejoiced and, being well pleased, he conceived the idea of making it more like its model. Accordingly, as that model is the ever-existent Living Being, he set about making the universe also like it, as far as possible, in that respect. Now the nature of that living Being was eternal, a character with which it was impossible fully to endow a generated thing. But he planned as it were a moving likeness of eternity; and, at the same time that he

---

[44] Fortune, D. *The Mystical Qabalah*, p. 59.

set in order the Heaven, he made, of eternity that abides in unity, an ever-flowing likeness moving according to number - that to which we have given the name Time.[45]

The idea that the universe is in the process of becoming increasingly real is also repeated in *The Unfinished Universe*, and one of the key implications of this meta-concept is referred to by Omar Khayyam in the *Rubaiyat*:

> With Earth's first clay they did the last man knead,
>
> And then of the last harvest sow'd the seed;
>
> Yea, the first morning of creation wrote
>
> What the last dawn of reckoning shall read.

This is reflected in Kabbalah by the statement that *Kether* contains the whole potential of manifestation within it. That is to say, due to the holographic nature of the universe, the pattern exists as a fundamental, implicit structure, at all levels, and is therefore immanent.

Carl Sagan uses this philosophy wonderfully in his fiction *Contact*, where the heroine finds, by using a computer to arrange the infinite regressions of the number Pi in base 11 arithmetic, "a miracle - another circle, drawn kilometres downstream of the decimal point".[46] He calls it the "Artist's Signature", and again we return to the idea of the recursive Universe, where the ripples of the thought of God form patterns always showing the way home.

The Tree as a Communications System (Lattice Theory)
I will briefly mention here that another of the implications of the Recursive Metaconcept in its relation to the Tree, and as rediscovered in modern quantum theory, is the so-called "Butterfly

---

[45] Plato, *Timaeus*, pp. 30-1.
[46] Sagan, C. *Contact*, p. 429.

effect" as found by Lorenz in weather pattern modelling. In poetic terms, as Francis Thompson put it in *The Mistress of Vision*:

"Thou canst not stir a flower

Without troubling of a star."

This idea basically states that it is impossible to predict the behaviour of a system due to the number of potential variables that can eventually cause, with very minute original change, large divergences in the possible emergent patterns. This is important in freeing the mind of the Magician from slavishly adhering to what have previously been considered immutable laws which are in effect merely habits of nature. It is this very principle that has helped examine, and at the same time, confound the "greenhouse effect" and global warming. The Magician must remain open to possibilities and opportunities that those blinded by expectation cannot see, and this is depicted by the Fool card of the tarot, who should be considered the esoteric emblem of the New Physics.

Another extension of the Lattice idea is that of the link between macrocosm and microcosm, the "greater" world and the "lesser" world. It can be seen that if the whole Universe is modelled as a latticework of reflective spheres, each point in the Universe reflects everything else. Thus, if a change occurs within one sphere, the whole is equally changed, and if a change occurs across wider areas of the lattice, then equally, every discrete point will be changed in reflection. This model is a more holistic vision of the many levels model previously adopted by some esoteric writers, which is more linear in that one world tends to be seen above or about the other. "As above, so below" can be equally considered as "as within, so without", or even, "as here, so everywhere".

Perhaps we can also see this pattern at work in that minute accidents of fate are often more influential in the causing of large divergences of personal and world history than pre-arranged grand events organised specifically to alter such things. Examples include the vision of the Roman Emperor Constantine, which radically affected the history of the world by his subsequent consolidation of Christianity as state religion for Rome from circa 325 AD, or the assassination of the Austrian politician which sparked the First World War.

This idea is used to effect in many fiction books, notably *The Muller-Fokker Effect* by John Sladek, *The Stochastic Man* by Robert Silverberg, and the *Illuminati* trilogy by Robert Anton Wilson and Robert Shea. The Magician can tremble such a web of recursion to great effect, as Marlowe says in *Dr Faustus*:

> The iterating of these lines brings gold;
>
> The framing of this circle on the ground
>
> Brings whirlwinds, tempests, thunder and lightning.[47]

---

[47] *The Tragical History of the Life and Death of Doctor Faustus*, Christopher Marlowe (1604), Scene V.

EXERCISES

1. Drawing the Tree of Life.

Stage One.

First, draw a straight vertical line down the centre of your sheet of paper. Ensure that the line is drawn in pencil as you will be erasing it once the basis structure has been drawn.

Stage 2.

Next, draw a circle whose top edge touches the top of the line, and whose lower edge comes to about one third of the way down the line. Draw another circle of the same size whose top edge touches the bottom of the first circle.

Stage 3.

Draw two further circles of the same size, the first using the intersection of the circles in stage two as a centre, and the second having a top edge which touches the bottom of the circle just drawn.

Stage Four.

You now have the centre points of each of the ten *Sephiroth* marked out, and can draw smaller circles to represent these as shown.

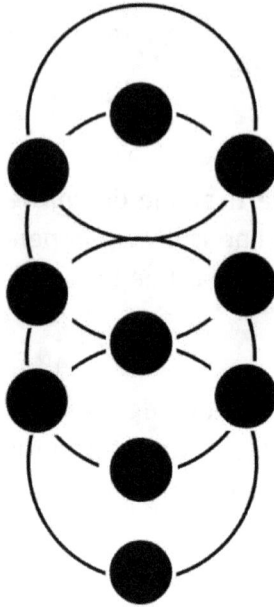

Illus. Drawing the Tree of Life Stage 4.

Stage Five.

Erase the drawing lines.

Stage Six.

Now connect the *Sephiroth* with the twenty-two paths, as shown. It may be easiest to begin with to draw the three vertical lines first, the three horizontal lines second, and then the diagonal lines third.

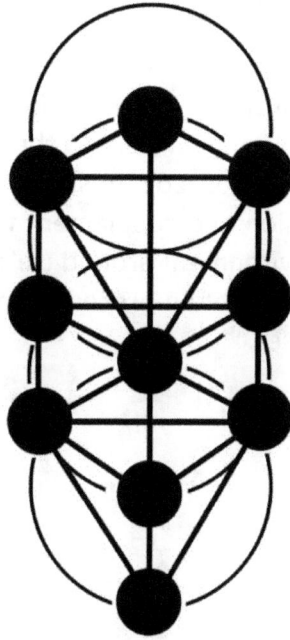

Illus. Drawing the Tree of Life Stage 6.

2. Collect examples of different orders of patterns. For example, choose a pattern such as; circles, curves, squares, sprays, or all ascending patterns. Then make a scrapbook of pictures, words and notes relating to this pattern. If you had chosen a triangle, you may be able to find pictures in magazines, a poem about three people, a diagram of a bridge support, and a picture of a star constellation in the form of a triangle. Use this exercise to demonstrate that the complex world about us can be seen to be composed of simple patterns in different orders. The simplest pattern, of course, is a point, which is a title of *Kether*.

3. Find a picture of something which for you symbolises an emanative system, i.e. a waterfall, an explosion, a flowchart, a flower. Meditate on this symbol at the start of each day, as a

reminder of the constant emanation taking place about, within and through you.

4. Observe ways in which we organise things; linear progressions, sets, sorts, orders, levels and layers, and the criteria we use to make sense of the world around us; colour, size, shape, number. Consider Kabbalah as an extension and supplement to the way in which we naturally order the environment around us. This ordering also takes place automatically as the brain processes the results of our vision, hearing and other senses.[48]

---

[48] To explore colour symbolism in the Kabbalah, see Sturzaker, D. & Sturzaker, J. *Colour and the Kabbalah*.

The Sephiroth and the Four Worlds

As discussed in the first chapter, each *Sephirah* on the Tree of Life descends into itself in an infinite regression, creating a recursive fractal pattern. However, each *Sephirah* within itself contains a complex of aspects. Whilst these appear quite technical and somewhat arbitrary divisions on first sight, it allows us to perceive nuances in the way events unfold, patterns emerge in nature, and in people's characters – or our own.

We will list below and briefly explore these six aspects of the *Sephiroth* as well as give a few examples of how this allows us to deepen our appreciation of the world through the map. It is like having a new overlay in more detail to our existing map, such as adding contours to a simple map, or perhaps even like having the floor plans of every building on a town map.

This complex sub-system within each *Sephirah* was developed by Cordovero and is known as the doctrine of the *behinot*, the infinite number of aspects which can be differentiated within each of the *Sephiroth*.[49]

As these aspects are rarely (if at all) covered in western esoteric or New Age books on Kabbalah, I have also attempted to provide a simple title for each of the aspects. These are obviously not from traditional schools of Kabbalah but given as a contemporary anchor for these very detailed aspects of the tradition.

1. The Attractor Aspect

A concealed aspect that exists even before its manifestation or emanation as a Sephirah.

If we see the *Sephiroth* as prisms reflecting the light in ways particular to their own structure, we can see that each prism is equally a limited perspective, a layer of reality convenient to the purposes of conceptualisation. That we have split the Universe and all that composes us, whether it is a concept such as revenge, an

---

[49] Scholem, G. *Kabbalah*, p. 114.

object such as a cheese-grater, or a process such as condensation, into ten generalised views should indicate that the ultimate aspect of that view must return to the unknown from which it was generated. This can be demonstrated by asking a simple question such as "why is that computer in this room?" which leads to a further "why did I buy it?", and so on in an infinite regress. Take the question "What is ...?" and a similar regression can be found. We can never know what a thing is, or why, and it is this same unknowable that lies at the heart of each of the *Sephiroth*. This also demonstrates how the *Sephiroth* proceed from *Ain Soph Aur*, and yet still reside within it.

2. The Apparent Aspect

The manifest and apparent aspect in its emanation as a Sephirah.

The form of a *Sephiroth* is represented by its name, and hence the apparent aspect and main form of *Yesod* is "foundation". Within any system to which the Tree is applied, the "foundation" will be *Yesod*. Again, splitting the Universe into ten aspects of its manifestation is probably based purely on our propensity as ten-digited beings to count in decimal. However, this does seem to work and orders of "ten" are found at many levels of the Universe around us. The concept should be applied in its most general sense, in that *Chesed* is not merely "loving kindness", but also the "expansive" aspect of any system.

3. The Active Aspect

The aspect in which it materialises its own location, i.e. the Sephirah itself.

The *Yesod* of manifestation can be seen in the foundation of all events, concepts and objects, for example the foundations of a building, the founding of a company, or the personality that nature and nuture provides us as the foundation of our self-identity.

There are three further aspects of each *Sephirah* that relate to the networked structure of the Tree. A *Sephirah* cannot be seen merely in terms of itself, but also must be viewed as part of a holistic system. A Spinning Wheel has one meaning in a Casino, where it is part of a financial system, and another in a Windmill, where it is part of a production system. The context in which a *Sephirah* is viewed is one of its aspects;

4. The Responsive Aspect

The aspect which enables the Sephirah above it to instil within it the power to emanate further Sephirah.

This is the receptive aspect of the *Sephirah*, which reflects its qualities in terms of those *Sephiroth* within the process which come before it. Thus, *Hod* has an aspect whereby *Geburah*, *Tiphareth* and *Netzach* instil within it an ability to continue the process by generating *Yesod*.

5. The Core Aspect

The aspect by which it gains the power to emanate the Sephiroth within it to their manifested existence within its own essence.

This is the central aspect of the node of activity, whereby it coalesces its own nature and from that proceeds forwards in the system. It is somewhat like the sudden chemical reaction which takes place in the slow mixture of two liquids when they reach the saturation point. Sometimes, this point of the process then begins a new reaction, such as the crystallisation of a solid, or the violent emission of heat.

6. The aspect by which the following *Sephirah* is emanated to its own place.

This is the transmitting aspect of the *Sephirah*, by which it governs the nature of the next *Sephirah* in the process. Obviously, the transmission or outflowing of a *Sephirah* is bound to shape the next, although in the networked nature of the Tree, each of the *Sephiroth* is more truly created by a conflux of prior *Sephiroth*, and result as their convergence.

As an example, *Tiphareth* (sometimes called the 'son'), is the result of the convergence of *Kether, Chockmah, Binah, Chesed* and *Geburah*. A good example of this is *Da'ath*, 'knowledge', which is seen as the union of *Chockmah* and *Binah*, and sometimes depicted as a non-*Sephirah* on the Abyss which separates the upper three *Sephiroth* from the rest of the Tree.

In addition to this type of description, two other versions describe how each *Sephirah* exists as a vector (from the Latin, meaning a 'bearer' or 'carrier') of the Light. The first details how light is reflected from each *Sephirah* back to the preceding *Sephirah*, as well as the light "flowing" downwards, as an object reflects light back to a torch, for example.

The second uses the premise of 'channels' (*zinnor*) that form between each *Sephirah*, apart from the emanative process, in that they model reciprocal influence between the *Sephiroth*, and not the lightning flash itself. This doctrine is more in accord with the standard occult map of the paths of the Tree of Life.

The Four Worlds
One of the fundamental concepts of Kabbalah is that of the existence of a number of worlds. This can range from the millions of worlds depicted as the strands of the beard of the long face of God, to the aborted worlds which preceded our own and referred to as the Kings of Edom (see the later chapter on the *Klippoth*). We can perhaps make a parallel of this concept to modern physics, and the Cophenhagen Interpretation with its many observer-created worlds.

A common understanding of these variations of the many-worlds doctrine came around the 14th century, but is also mentioned in the *Zohar*, and was developed primarily by the Lurianic school in the 16th century.

This version depicted four worlds:

> (a) *Olam ha-azilut*, the world of emanation (the *Sephiroth*)

(b) *Olam ha-beriah*, the world of creation (the Throne & Chariot)

(c) *Olam ha-yezirah*, the world of formation (the Angels)

(d) *Olam ha-asiyyah*, the world of making (the terrestrial sphere)

The four worlds can be connected with the four letters of the divine name YHVH, the four quarters, the four elements, and other quaternary systems. They can be further described as:

(a) *Azilut [Atziluth]*, the world of emanations, at which level that which renders possibility becomes real (i.e. the thirty-two paths of wisdom).

(b) *Beriah [Briah]*, the world of creation, at which level the spirit is moved to general manifestation without differentiation. The *Zohar* calls this world the pavilion which veils the point.

(c) *Yetzirah*, the world of formation, the level at which the general spirit is broken down into a crowd of individual minds.

(d) *Assiyah [Assiah]*, the world of production.

In essence, the first world is that which is emanated directly from the divine source, falling into the process of creation in the second world or stage, then being formed into patterns in the third world and finally arriving at manifestation in the fourth and final world.

At each level the practical Kabbalist works with a different mode of personification of the Divine, in that at the world of *Assiah* he works with the elemental spirits, in the world of *Yetzirah* he works with the Angels, in the world of *Briah* the Archangels, and at the world of *Atziluth* he works directly with the ten names of God in each of the *Sephiroth*.

However, the basic idea is that the Universe is broken down into four layers of functionality, each of which resonates with the others. A more practical example of a "four worlds" application is in business planning, where the layers are seen as strategic, tactical, operational, and functional. A full business plan will integrate these layers by having a simple, but broad strategic goal, broken into tactical means of attaining this goal, each tactic being further analysed in terms of its operation, and then being applied in the day-to-day functioning of the business. The "worlds" must be consistent with each other to ensure the overall objective is reached - every function must be in line with the overall plan (or "that which is above is like unto that which is below").

There are three fundamental concepts underpinning the doctrine of the four worlds of Kabbalah, being the four-fold quaternary, the concept of hierarchy and the notion of the multiverse:

1. The Quaternary

The number four has a symbolic connection to the concepts of space, classification, and the physical world. It is seen in numerology as the number of order and relativity. It is the Cube or Altar upon which the Emperor (card IV of the tarot) is seated, dispensing order and form to the manifest world.

Jung saw the balanced quaternary (or Tetrad) as a fundamental pattern of thought, "... the quaternary is an archetype of almost universal occurrence. It forms the logical basis for any whole judgement. If one wishes to pass such judgement, it must have this fourfold aspect".[50] This Judgement is that made by *Geburah* once the first four *Sephiroth* are in place.

Rudy Rucker proposes the following conceptual tetrad to match the Jungian four modes, which I feel can be usefully referred to the four worlds as they exist in the psyche:

Number (Sensation) referred to *Assiah*.

---

[50] Jung, C. G. *Alchemical Studies*, p. 167.

Space (Feeling) referred to *Yetzirah*.

Logic (Thinking) referred to *Briah*.

Infinity (Intuition) referred to *Atziluth*.

The fifth concept, that of Information, can be seen (as the top point of the Pentagram or as the *Shin* descending into YHVH) as the binding or redeeming concept and may be referred to the divine presence in each of the worlds in terms of communication, complexity, and meaning.[51]

Information, in terms of coherence and organisation is resultant of the fact that "Life is an ordering, selecting, coherence-making process".[52] The physicist Schrödinger put it simply that "Life feeds on negative entropy".[53]

2. The Hierarchy

Briefly, the evidence for hierarchy as a fundamental part of the *scala natura* is constantly about and within us, from the hierarchy of the cells within us to the hierarchy of any organisation or the hierarchy of star systems. During a talk given at the Arcane School Conference, Mark Braham phrased it:

> Hierarchization is the process through which successive levels of increasing complexity, flexibility, and co-ordination in form, function and behaviour are established, ranging from the relatively simple to the relatively complex.[54]

The higher up the hierarchy an item or individual is, the more is their co-ordinating function on a scale of complexity (such as a Queen in a beehive, a Sun in a Solar System, or a Company Director). This is important to consider in defining which world is to

---

[51] Rucker, R. *Mind Tools*, pp. 19-20.
[52] Wilson, R. A. *Prometheus Rising*, p. 90.
[53] *Ibid*.
[54] Arcane School Conference talk notes, n.d. Also reproduced in *Beacon*, v52 i10 July-Aug, pub. Lucis Trust, p. 296.

be considered or worked with for the Practical Kabbalist. It may be that some contemplations or workings are best effected in *Assiah* or with the elemental beings and others more effective by working with the Archangels or the correspondences of *Briah*.

3. The Multiverse

The concepts involved with the Many Worlds or Copenhagen Interpretation of Quantum Physics can be reconciled with the Kabbalistic system through the nature of the four worlds and the description Kabbalah gives through Genesis. However, the basic idea of the multiverse is not new, and exists in many other cosmologies.

EXERCISES

1. Choose any real-life situation you are involved with, and separate it out into the four worlds as follows.

> **Atziluth**: What are the highest, most abstract, aspects of the situation? What are the principles involved if you were to dramatise the situation? Is it a situation of love, or honour, or money and pleasure? How does it relate to the evolution of our species? What spiritual impulses are there involved?

> **Briah**: What is the situation creating that wasn't there before? What new ideas, events, feelings, objects, points-of-view, movements of people are involved? Is it a very creative situation, or one that doesn't involve much change?

> **Yetzirah**: What forms and patterns are apparent in the situation? Does it have a regular, predictable, quality, or is it chaotic? Is it all over in a moment, or does it occur at intervals? What models could you apply to the situation; a psychological or sociological explanation, a political one, or even an old popular saying?

> **Assiah**: What happens, shorn of all the above? What actual events and behaviour take place without making any judgements of them? So, do not note that "Roger behaves angrily", but rather, "Roger shouts and makes noises by banging his fists on the table". This observation of Assiah without the other levels is a useful skill in itself, and occurs with people who make natural counsellors or investigators. It is in a sense like watching a television film without the sound; other aspects of the events become more noticeable than would otherwise be so.

Use the steps to observe whether each of the Worlds is being suitably and consistently with those preceding it. For example, is one of the events in Assiah is "People being late", and one of the aspects of Briah is "creation of an efficient workforce", then something is obviously wrong.

We will now look at each of the *Sephiroth* in isolation, defining their particular qualities and roles in the engine of creation and the ladder of ascension. This may at first appear an extended discussion of disparate pieces with little application to everyday life. However, we advise readers to persevere with getting to know each of the *Sephirah* individually and together in pairs, triads, and columns, illustrated by the tarot images on their connecting paths. As you build up each set a little, consider how they work down the Tree in terms of a process of creation and up the Tree in terms of learning and spiritual progression. Keep coming back to each piece like a jigsaw, trying to apply it to different aspects of life and eventually you will discover how it fits together, piece at a time.

Consider a work or personal project and place it on the Tree; would you say it would correspond to a *Kether* stage or a *Tiphareth* stage, a *Malkuth* stage or *Yesod*? Consider two people as two *Sephiroth* and look at the tarot card that illustrates their relationship. Consider the lessons you are repeatedly learning at a particular time of your life, and assign them to a *Sephirah*. What paths must you master below to be free to progress, and what paths above offer you that progress? Read Crowley and other esoteric writers and see how they have used Kabbalah to underpin their writings and how they thought about each of the *Sephiroth*. We have also provided a reading list for your further elaboration of the Tree. It should never be a dry learning of dissociated and inapplicable facts – the Tree is a living map of creation and our living journey within that creation. It is a lifetime activity.

For example, we could take dressmaking. *Kether* is the point at which it is decided that one wants to live in a world with a dress as against a world without one. Forces are then set in motion to bring this about (*Chockmah*), resulting in a form that describes that world (*Binah*). This is all carried out prior to conscious knowing, although that 'knowing' (*Da'ath*) can sometimes happen. Crossing the Abyss, these factors then create a vision (*Chesed*) which is received in awareness (*Tiphareth*), but must be balanced by previous experience of one's limitations (*Geburah*). *Tiphareth* must receive the influences of all these factors and transform them into drive and energy (*Netzach*) in the material world.

This must be balanced by planning (*Hod*) until a pattern for the dress is arrived at (*Yesod*). This pattern, if all the other stages have been adequately achieved, will contain everything necessary to create the dress. Finally, the dress will be made (*Malkuth*), fulfilling *Kether* and creating a world with a dress. Whether this matches the vision will depend on whether discipline and experience has been applied (the balance between *Chesed* and *Geburah*) and whether the energy has been efficient will be dependent on whether planning has been applied (the balance between *Netzach* and *Hod*).

We will begin our exploration of the individual *Sephiroth* with a necessary concept that is the most mystical of all concepts in Kabbalah – the *Ain Soph Aur*.

Ain Soph Aur: A Necessary Non-Negation

Kabbalah postulates that *Kether*, the point from which expansion began through the *Sephiroth* into existence, is in itself the *Malkuth* of a "negative existence", a limitless "being" which contracted to a point in *Kether*. *Kether* itself is the *Malkuth* of the absolutely unknowable, from which all things proceed. The infinite being is viewed as having three veils drawn above *Kether*, which cover its essential essence and by which it is known:

AIN	Nothing, nought
AIN SVPh	Infinite (SVTh - End)
AIN SVPh AVR	Limitless Light (AVR - Light, fire)

The neverness of AIN and its negativity is due in part to the infinite nature of the light, which is indefinable and hence negative to human consciousness. This aspect of divinity is examined in such mystical treatises as *The Cloud of Unknowing* and *The Ascent of Mount Carmel:*

> The divine darkness is the inaccessible light in which God is said to dwell (1 Timothy 6:10), invisible indeed, because of the superabundant light.[55]

In the temple the Initiate reminds themselves of this unknowable presence by the Lamp of Dazzling Darkness, which is the ever-burning and eternal lamp of Edessa, of Jupiter Ammon, of Pallas, and the perpetual lamp found in the tomb of Christian Rosencreutz. An alternative translation of *Ain Soph Aur* could be "never-ending fire", and Crowley may be hinting at this when he speaks of the Lamp:

> Eternal, unconfined, unextended, without cause and without effect, the Holy Lamp mysteriously burns. Without

---

[55] Walsh, J. (ed). *The Cloud of Unknowing*, fn. 435.

quantity or quality, unconditioned and sempiternal, is this Light.[56]

He later states that the Lamp "is before 'I am'", thus confirming that he is attributing it above *Kether* (whose God-name is EHIEH, "I am that I am") and therefore to the *Ain Soph Aur*.

In writing of AIN, Mathers notes "this word consists of three letters, which thus shadow forth the first three *Sephiroth* or numbers"[57]. I would like to examine this comment in more detail, as I believe it reveals much about that which cannot be spoken of except by analogy and forms the Triangle of the Unbeheld.

The three letters of Ain can be broken down as follows:

Aleph   Transcendence

Yod   Transition

Nun   Transformation

We might also consider these as illustrated by their corresponding tarot images of the Fool, Hermit and Death cards. The *Ain* is the negation of light in three different manners; the paradox of the Fool, the withdrawal of the Hermit, and the transformation of Death.

Aleph in Kether
The Ain, or "naught" is embodied in the sublime symbol of the Fool tarot card, the 'nought' card. However, it should be seen that the Fool is not a Zero in the same way that the *Ain* is negative rather than nothing. The negative in this case is that of the finite glyph of *Kether*, the point (having position but not magnitude) as created from the infinite *Ain* (having infinite magnitude and no position).

Kether can be represented as the God Hadit and the Ain represented by the Goddess Nuit in the Thelemic system developed

---

[56] Crowley, A. *Magick*, p. 104.
[57] Mathers S. L. M., *The Kabbalah Unveiled*, p. 20.

by Aleister Crowley. In Magick, Chapter 0 (hence, the Ain) he states "Infinite space is called the Goddess Nuit, while the infinitely small and atomic yet omnipresent point is called Hadit".[58] This is the basis of all Cosmology, which refers to the known, the unknown, and ultimately, their interaction.

Yod in Chockmah

The first swirlings of *Chockmah* can be seen as the shadowing of both the *Yod* of AIN and the stage of AIN SVPh in the three veils. The masculine potency of this *Sephirah*, in its position at the top of the positive pillar, can also be seen in the glyph of *Yod* as representing either the hand or the seed. In the symbol of the hand we see the movement and sign of action as *Kether* expands forth into the explosion or big bang of *Chockmah*.

As the seed, *Yod* represents the principle of all things, potential in the *Aleph* of *Kether*, (the value of 1), but now expanding through the action represented by *Chockmah* and the number 10, value of *Yod*, being the number of *Sephiroth* in the full Tree of Life. It is important to note that Kabbalists state that the thirty-two paths of wisdom derive from *Chockmah*, which as a reflection of *Ain Soph* would correlate in that the paths could not emanate from the *Kether* stage in that *Ain* is naught, but would have to expand from the *Ain Soph* stage where the naught is progressed to the not-naught.

Also, it is stated that the "1" of *Kether* cannot become anything in that it is the Unity, and thus only through its own reflection (the formula of 1+1=2, rather than the mystic formula of 0=2) as the "2" of *Chockmah* can manifestation begin. In the light of progress up the tree (the initiatory system), then the SVPh stage of *Chockmah* is the "end" as the grade of *Ipssissimus* in *Kether* is "wholly free of all limitations soever" as Crowley puts it.[59]

---

[58] Crowley, A. *Magick*, p. 143.
[59] *Ibid*, p. 329.

Nun in Binah

At the creative stage represented by *Binah*, the *Sephirah* at the top of the negative Pillar of Form, we see "shadowed forth" the *Nun* of AIN and the final veil of AIN SVPh AVR. It is obvious that an immediate connection can be made in that the value of NVN is fifty, and from *Binah* are derived the "fifty gates of Understanding".

NVN is primarily the letter of transformation, and the Scorpio energy in Astrology. It thus signifies change of form, which at its highest level depends on *Binah*, the mother of all Form. Also in *Binah* we see the AVR stage of the three veils, although the AVR, or light, is perceived as the blackness of the bitter sea of *Binah* because its limitlessness is impossible for understanding to contain.

The value of AIN SVPH AVR by *Gematria* is 1586, which reduces to 1+5+8+6 = 20 = 2+0 = 2, thus resuming the formula of 0=2, which is more fully stated as 0 = n + (-n), or perhaps NOTHING = SELF + GOD (the infinitely small point of self when attempted to be perceived by consciousness, and the infinitely large presence of God when attempted to be perceived likewise).

Broken down, the AIN has the value of 511, which is of intense significance in the cult of *Thelema*, in that it equals 418 + 93, which are the numbers of the Great Work, and the Current that informs it.

It is also the value of A'aBVDH H-TYTh, "the worship of the snake" (that is, the Snake of Wisdom coiled up the Tree of Life). Note also that 511 reduces to 7, the number of the card to which the Graal (and hence 418) is attributed, the Chariot. As Kate Bush sings in *Sat in your Lap* (from the album, *The Dreaming*):

> "I hold a CUP of WISDOM (*Binah* and *Chockmah*), but there is NOTHING within"

Which is to state, Kabbalistically, that *Binah* is the final shadowing forth of the three negative veils of AIN SOPH AUR.

SVPh has the value of 868, which breaks down to 22 (the number of paths on the Tree) and 2+2 = 4, which is to say that the SVPh, or "end" is in the creative process actually the beginning of the material world (4, the number of materialisation) from *Chockmah*, to which I have attributed SVPh. Note that again it is also the reflection of itself (2+2 = 4) in order to manifest.

AVR, the light has the value of 207, which reduces to 9, the number of *Teth*, the Snake of Wisdom. Thus, the Light and the Snake are brought together (as the Zorastorian verse reads, "... that fire that darts and flashes throughout the hidden depths of the Universe..") The number 418 is the value of KBVD ZYV H-NChSh, "the bright glory of the snake", and hence the Great Work completed as the Snake reaches *Kether* and the Light floods down it.

The word RBH, meaning 'archer' has the value of 207, showing the process of shooting up the Middle Pillar of the Tree in the mystical process of attaining the AVR rather than the magical one of ascending back up the Lightning Flash.

Having looked briefly at this mystical concept of *Ain Soph Aur*, we will now turn to *Kether*, the point which is created from this contraction of nothingness, and how *Kether* emanates into manifestation through the further nine *Sephiroth* in turn.

EXERCISES

1. Light a candle in a darkened room, and stand or sit back from it. Imagine that the Tree of Life is the candle itself, and the flame is *Kether*. Try to visualise as strongly as possible the darkness of the room "contracting" itself to create the point of light, turning inside-out your first perception that the light is radiating into the darkness. This simple meditation may assist an experiential awareness of what is essentially the highest knowable aspect of the Tree of Life.

2. You will need a tarot pack for this exercise. The Waite-Smith Tarot deck, or any modern pack based on those designs is a standard choice, or the more adventurous may select the Thoth deck by Crowley, or any of the hundreds of variants available. It is obviously preferable that the pack was designed with the Kabbalah

in mind. An Arthurian or Aztec pack might yield some surprising insights, but these will be easier to gain from a more standard design. Take the cards which have the letters of AIN attributed to them:

Aleph: FOOL

Yod: HERMIT

Nun: DEATH

What feelings and thoughts arise when contemplating these images? What do they indicate about the Kabbalistic concept of AIN?

Kether: The Crown of Coherent Light

The Doctrine of Trans-Resonance

One of the primary doctrines of Magick we refer to throughout this book is "that which is above is like unto that which is below", also stated as "the heaven is in the earth, but after an earthly manner; and that the earth is in the heaven, but after a heavenly manner," or Kabbalistically as "*Malkuth* is in *Kether*, and *Kether* is in *Malkuth*, but after another manner."

This doctrine of what we might refer to as trans-resonance is presented in Kabbalah as an intimate and ultimate identity between *Malkuth* and *Kether*, the most mundane and the most mystical of the *Sephiroth*. We can examine aspects of this resonance by a method known as permutation, combining the Hebrew letters of both words. If the letters of *Kether* (KThR) and *Malkuth* (MLKVTh) are merged together and matched in pairs, the resultant Hebrew words are:

MR: The Hebrew for Myrrh, the resin of suffering and sorrow, used for anointing (the head or feet, attributed to *Kether* and *Malkuth*) and embalming (the body, attributed as a whole to *Malkuth*). Also symbolic of the suffering endured in the separation of *Malkuth* and *Kether* from each other by the Fall.

RM: Meaning "High, exalted", both attributes of *Kether*, and also meaning to decay (worm-eaten), thus the process of Malkuth and the decay implicit in evolution symbolised by the Worm, Dragon or Serpent. It can be noted that a rearrangement of the letters of KThR gives KRTh, meaning "to cut off", and "divine punishment", perhaps indicating that any deviation from the Crown brings about a Fall from the state of Grace represented by *Kether*.

KL: Meaning "to comprehend, measure, all every, whole, any", referring to *Kether* as the All and the highest comprehension - the "Admirable Intelligence" as the *Sepher Yetzirah* entitles it. Also "Invisible Intelligence" in that if something is everything, it cannot ever be perceived because there is nowhere outside it to perceive it from. Thus, "occult" and "unspeakable" experiences are so because they defy comprehension as they partake of this ultimate ground of reality.

LK: A word meaning "to you" and hence can be seen as the mystical return up the Tree of Life from *Malkuth* to *Kether* as the "you" is the Self, or God one is moving towards.

K: The letter *Kaph*, the Hand of God in *Kether*, "who hath measured the waters in the hollow of his hand and meted out heaven with the span" - Isaiah 40, v.12. Also the hand as the receptive *Malkuth* on the Tree. The symbolism of the Hand is varied, but in this context can be seen as representing the transmission of divine grace between *Kether* and *Malkuth*. Also see notes later referring to *Kaph* and the Wheel tarot card as attributed to *Kether*.

ThV: *Tau*, the cross and synthesis in *Malkuth*, but also symbolic of spirit (the "crown", or *Kether* of the Pentagram) crucified in the four elements (comprising *Malkuth*).

Th: The letter *Tau*, as described above. It also represents a boundary, which could be described as *Malkuth* being the ultimate boundary of *Kether*, or Mark, in that *Malkuth* is the visible aspect of *Kether*.

Numerically, *Malkuth* values 496, which totals to 19 (4+9+6), which totals to 10 (1+9), which can be broken down to 1 as well. Thus, *Malkuth* (10) and *Kether* (1) are within the value of *Malkuth* itself. *Kether*, on the other hand, values 620 (the *Zohar* speaks of the 620 pillars of light), which breaks down to 8 (6+2), the number of the *Sephirah Hod*. This is an interesting attribution in respect of the initiatory experiences associated with *Hod* in the Grade of Practicus of the Golden Dawn system.

A final point using *Gematria* is that the value of the word 'Swan', the symbolic bird of *Kether* and illumination, is BRBVR = 410, which is also the value of Magic (MQA'aR) and the 'Confession of God's Unity' (the Shema, ShMA'a).

The Triune Crown

The Triple Crown worn by the Pope can be viewed as representing the Trinity of *Kether* extended in itself, *Chockmah* and *Binah*, for above the Abyss the *Sephiroth* merge with each other in the same way that the four lower *Sephiroth* below the Veil merge within *Malkuth*.

We can make a correspondence of the three letters of KThR to the first three *Sephiroth* (including itself) as follows:

Kaph: *Kether*

Tau: *Chockmah*

Resh: *Binah*

A further breakdown is utilised by spelling the letters again in full. The tarot cards to which these letters are assigned offer valuable descriptions of the nature of this creative trinity of Forces.

Kaph in Kether

Kaph, as previously described, is the hand of God transmitting the vital spark to Man, and the hand of Man receiving the divine influx (as painted on the ceiling of the Sistine Chapel by Michelangelo, for example). Its tarot glyph is that of the Wheel, a symbol of synchronicity, *Kether* being the pivot and *Malkuth* being the hub. The number of the card is 10, referring to the number of *Malkuth*, the number of *Sephiroth* contained within *Kether*, and reducing to 1, the unity of *Kether* itself.

Spelt in full, *Kaph* is *Kaph + Peh*, corresponding to the Wheel and the Blasted Tower, each of which can be seen as a process of evolution. On the one hand, progressive and cyclic, on the other hand, sudden and decisive. In terms of *Kether* we see in these cards the doctrine of Unity in Diversity (the spindle and spokes of the wheel) implicit in *Kether*, and the doctrine of the breaking of the shells in Lurianic Kabbalah (the tower or 'blasted house' being matter struck by the lightning flash of creation).

Tau in Chockmah

Tau is attributed to the Universe card, and we can see that the Universal creation implicit in *Kether* as potential is first given expansion in *Chockmah*. As symbolic of manifestation, the Universe card depicts *Chockmah* as the first manifestation of Unity, the visibility of *Kether* in the first swirling of the *Primum Mobile*, the Zodiac. The Golden Dawn tarot card depicts the spheres of the zodiac arranged around the central figure of the Atu (see later chapter for further explanations of the creative process of *Chockmah* as depicted by the Zodiac).

Spelt in full, *Tau* is *Tau* + *Vau*, corresponding to the Universe and the Hierophant. This affirms the Hierophant as symbolic of God's Wisdom (the translation of *Chockmah* being 'wisdom') and as the Interface between God (*Kether*) and the rest of Creation (*Binah to Malkuth*). This idea is mirrored in that the attribution of YHVH to the *Sephiroth* links *Kether* to *Chockmah* as the upper and lower parts of the *Yod*, *Binah* as *Heh*, the central *Sephiroth* to *Vau* (centred on *Tiphareth*, the Son) and *Malkuth* being the final *Heh* (the daughter that must be redeemed to *Binah*, the mother).

Thus, on the progression up the Tree, *Malkuth* (the Universe) must be raised to *Binah* (Transcendent Understanding) which is the state of the *Magister Templi* in the WEIS (attributed to *Binah*), who tends his temple and garden comprising the *Sephiroth* below the Abyss.

This develops into a state where the understanding becomes a mirror of the divine will and the mystic achieves *Chockmah* by becoming a pure interface to God. Finally, the Way is completed (*Yod* as symbolic of the Way depicted on the Hermit tarot card) by recognising the unity of all things, and hence the same letter covers both *Kether* and *Chockmah*. The Hermit tarot card to which *Yod* is attributed is also associated with the Neophyte ceremony of the Golden Dawn, and demonstrates that even from the first step on the path, the goal is always already there if we could but be aware of it.

Resh in Binah

Resh refers to consciousness and light through the tarot card of the Sun, and in the context of *Binah* affirms that the three supernal *Sephiroth* reside in the 'white head' (*Resh* means 'head') of *Kether*. The hemispheres of the brain may be divided into *Chockmah* and *Binah*, whilst the crown of the head is *Kether*. The Greater and Lesser Holy Assemblies of the *Zohar* elaborate on this symbolism at length.

Resh is also (via the Sun tarot card) allocated to *Tiphareth*, symbolic of consciousness and is the state of mind dealt with physically by the 'front of the head' (a more accurate translation of *Resh*). It can be deduced from this current attribution that understanding is a transcendent form of consciousness (the Sun of *Tiphareth* arising from the Sea of *Binah* as the Golden Dawn image depicts it) preceding the final synthesis in *Chockmah* of the Magician before God.

This is resumed under the symbolism of the Bornless Ritual as recorded by Aleister Crowley in *Liber Samekh*.[60] The original Greek text of the ritual (*Fragments of a Graeco-Egyptian work upon magic*, trans. Goodwin 1852) uses the phrase 'the headless one', or 'the headless spirit', but the Hebrew would be AChD BAIN RASh or AChD BLA RASH, meaning 'one without a head'. This is likely to have been utilised by Crowley in his re-naming of the rite as that of the bornless one, i.e. one without a beginning, as *Resh* can mean 'beginning' as well as 'head', as in BRAShITh, 'in the beginning', the first word of Genesis.

Traditional Kabbalah attributes the 'B' to *Kether*, and the 'RAShITh' to *Chockmah*, but it could also be seen that the *Beth* refers to the *Ain Soph Aur*, and hence the *Resh* to *Kether*, the *Yod* to the *Sephiroth* from *Binah* to *Yesod*, and the final *Tau* to *Malkuth*.

---

[60] Crowley, A. *Magick*, p. 355.

The *Kabbalistic Diagrams of Rosenroth* also refer to the "head which is not", or "the head of not", in Aramaic RIShA DLA. Indeed, one part of this text states quite clearly:

> The crown of the Holy King, which is called the Head which is Not, and the Head of knowing and not being known ... and is called the Ancient Concealed One.

Thus, the Bornless Ritual is an ascent up the middle pillar of consciousness from the bound lights of *Malkuth* and ultimately, to the boundless light of the *Ain Soph Aur*.

Resh spelt in full is *Resh + Yod + Shin*, and relates to the cards of the Sun, Hermit and Last Judgement. These could be transliterated into the phrase "The Awareness (Sun) of the True (Hermit) Will (Judgement)", which takes place in the initiation process at two key points, the first on crossing the Veil and attaining to *Tiphareth*, and the second on crossing the Abyss and attaining to the *Sephirah Binah*. The following extensions can be drawn:

> Will in *Malkuth*: The Way of Nature, the "entelechy" of Aristotle in the unfolding of blossoms and the formation of galaxies. The "selfish gene" or "blind watchmaker" aspect of nature in the unfolding genesis about us.

> Will in *Yesod*: The Way of the Personality, an understanding of the ego requirements, cultural conditioning and so forth. The development of purpose, aim, goal, valuation, motivation and intention through a discipline such as Psychosynthesis.

> Will in *Tiphareth*: The Way of the Self. The Individual Will of the transcendent Self in recognition of the lower *Sephiroth*. Also the "way of the burning heart", and surrender to the "Inner Voice", "Higher Self", or Will of Christ.

> Will in *Kether*: The Way of God. The Universal Will, the Will of God, the state of Unity where it is "thus so". The Taoist "action by non-action", and the Way of the Siddhis.

The Tree of Crowns

In ritual, the *Kether* of each *Sephiroth* can be represented by the headdress worn by the participant. I offer here a list of those I have allocated, but it is by no means exhaustive and would obviously also be dependent on the symbolism adopted by the ritual participant:

Kether: A Circlet of Gold or Ritual Crown. The Parsley Crown of the Nemean Games, sacred to Zeus.

Chockmah: The Twin Feathers, or Crown of Thoth.

Binah: The Crimson cap of concealment.

Chesed: The Cardinals hat, or Emperors Crown. The Pine Crown of the Isthmian games, sacred to Poseidon.

Geburah: The War Helm, or Martial Crown. The Judges Wig.

Tiphareth: The Solar Crown, Cowl, or the Wimple. The Crown of Thorns. The Roman Crown of Roses.

Netzach: The Laurel Wreath of Victory.

Hod: The Caduceus Crown or the Mortar Board.

Yesod: Crowns of disguise; wigs and masques. The Lunar Crown.

Malkuth: The Skull Cap. The Crown of Wild Olives of the Olympian games, sacred to Zeus. The Wreath. Crown of flowers, or ears of corn or wheat. Shamanic headdress composed of earth attributes.

In ritual, you could also correspond the Egyptian Crowns that symbolised the gods and goddesses to the *Sephiroth* with the following correspondences:

Kether: Pthah

Chockmah: Ma'at

Binah: Nuit, Isis

Chesed: Amoun

Geburah: Horus

Tiphareth: Osiris

Netzach: Hathor

Hod: Thoth

Yesod: Khons, Shu

Malkuth: Nekhbet

This further demonstrates how Kabbalah and correspondences can be used to build up ritual format and content.

EXERCISES

1. Take any process, and ask "What is the point of this act?" or "What is the aim of this event?" The answer should not only contain the purpose or result of the act, but you will observe it contains the source for the act as well, if not directly, and then implied. This demonstrates the state relationship between *Kether* and *Malkuth*, where *Kether* is the source and the aim, *Malkuth* the result and the action, and both are ultimately identical.

2. Take any dysfunctional process, or act which is not achieving the desired aim, and analyse it in terms of the letters which compose *Kether*:

> *Kaph*: The timing of the events within the process.
>
> *Tau*: The beliefs underpinning the process.
>
> *Resh*: The Awareness of the event, the thoughts and feelings you have.

Attempt to elevate each of these letters to the *Sephirah* to which each letter is attributed in the Triune Crown of *Kether*:

> **Kaph** (**Kether**): Ensure that the timing moves towards a focused point.
>
> **Tau** (**Chockmah**): Ensure that your beliefs are formed in wisdom, that is, applied experience.
>
> **Resh** (**Binah**): Ensure that you have understanding, i.e., being aware of the whole form.

This is an example of the way in which combinations of the letters and *Sephiroth* can be used to elevate mundane acts to their optimum potential.

Chockmah: The Quarry of Devotion

Chockmah, meaning "wisdom", is the second *Sephirah* in the lightning-flash descent of the Tree of Life, and takes its place at the top of the positive pillar. It is negative only in respect of *Kether*, from whom it receives its influence (*Mezla*), and positive in respect of *Binah*, 'Understanding', the third *Sephirah*. It connects in the Golden Dawn model (based on Kircher) to *Kether*, *Binah*, *Tiphareth* and *Chesed*, and the linking paths have the following tarot cards attributed to them; Fool, Empress, Emperor, and the Hierophant.

In the *Berakhot* (7a), it is written "the beginning of thought, and the first revelation of the array, is the second *Sefirah*, which is called *Chockmah*-Wisdom", and in the *Sepher Yetzirah*, *Chockmah* is more fully defined as "the Illuminating Intelligence, the Crown of Creation, the splendour of Unity, equalling it. It is exalted above every head, and is named by Kabbalists the Second Glory".

Chockmah is essentially the concept of force, dynamism, and energy, as this "first revelation of the array". It is the extension of the point of *Kether*, which was contracted from the *Ain*, into manifestation - as a line. In terms of Astrophysics this process took place a ten-millionth of a quadrillionth of a sextillionth second after the explosion of the singularity of *Kether*. The fundamental forces of Nature were tied together in one superforce. These forces are now defined in some models as; Electromagnetism, Weak force, Strong Force, and Gravity. These are seen as acting in ten possible dimensions, which neatly mirrors the Kabbalistic scheme of the four elements and the ten *Sephiroth*.

In Theological terms, *Chockmah* represents the *Logos*, the Divine Word or Will. All that was potential in *Kether* is now directed, and what was merely location now has direction. Logos translates as either Word or Thought, and hence is taken as the self-expression of God. In Heraclitus, Logos is the underlying balance or rationality in the manifest world of flux. The Stoics took this idea as the Reason of the Universe, God. The divine plan for which mystics search has its place in *Chockmah*, the layer of the creative process wherein the lattice or array is formed.

Many Jewish thinkers, on the other hand, identified the Logos with Wisdom, and the *Memra*, or Word. John 1:1 states "In the beginning was the Logos", and the *Wisdom of Solomon* says "Like a fine mist she [wisdom] rises from the power of God ... she is the reflection of the everlasting Light ... herself unchanging, but makes all things new ... she spans the world from end to end, and orders all things benignly."

In the *Sefer HaPardes*, it is noted that *Chockmah* is called Fear, as *Geburah* is also entitled *Pachad*, or fear. Whereas the fear of *Geburah* is the fear of the "vengeful lord", the fear spoken of in *Chockmah* is the mystical fear, which is that when the contemplative's thoughts reach this high place, a place without measure or boundary, where the mind does has no power to grasp. The relationship between *Chockmah* and *Geburah* demonstrates the Kabbalistic concept that the *Sephiroth* form arcs to each other, so that aspects of *Chockmah* can be seen in both *Geburah* and *Hod* and aspects of *Binah* seen both through *Chesed* and *Netzach*.

As stated in Job 28:28, "He says to man, behold the fear of God is Wisdom, and to depart from evil is understanding." This indicates, in terms of the ascent of the Tree, that *Binah* (Understanding) is above the Abyss, wherein one departs from the evil of the separate worlds, and that *Chockmah* (Wisdom) is the last step to *Kether* (God).

In Hebrew, *Chockmah*, 'wisdom', is spelt *Cheth + Kaph + Mem + Heh*, transliterated as ChKMH. The letters have the following correspondences according to Levi:

Ch:	Distribution	Single
K:	Force (Wealth, according to Papus)	Double
M:	Death (Water)	Mother

The distributive aspect of *Chockmah* is in its reception and transmission of the light of *Kether*. Indeed, *Chockmah* is that process in itself, and thus recurs at all levels of the Tree. The double letter *Kaph* also directly mirrors the nature of *Chockmah* in its attribute of force, and indicates that the nature of that force is circular in its connection to the Wheel Atu of the tarot. *Mem*, subtitled 'Death' in this scheme, indicates that *Chockmah* is the first and last *Sephiroth* that can be known - due to *Kether* having no other reference outside itself. As religion, *Heh* refers to the perfect Path of *Yod* flowing down the Tree as the Tao from *Chockmah*, or the strait gate and narrow way; "Because strait is the gate, and narrow is the way, which leadeth unto life, and few there be that find it" [Matthew 7:14].

In the derivation of the channels, *Cheth* is the God of Mercy; *Kaph*, God the Immutable; *Mem*, God the Arcane; and *Heh*, God of God.

Another explanation gives:

Ch: Allocated to *Chesed*, produces the animals

K: The description assigned to *Kaph* by Papus is worth quoting in full:

> Designates the first heaven, corresponding to the name of God *Yod* expressed in one letter, that is the primary cause which sets all that is mobile in movement...govern[s] the sky of the fixed stars, notably the twelve signs of the Zodiac which the Hebrews call *Galgol hamnazeloth*; the intelligence of the second heaven is called Raziel. His attribute signifies the vision of God and the smile of God.[61]

M: Allocated to *Chesed* and *Geburah*.

---

[61] Papus, *The Qabalah*, p. 102.

H: Attributed to *Geburah*, force and power, the numeration being *Pachad* (*Peh* + *Cheth* + *Daleth*), fear and judgement.

The divine name of *Chockmah* (or embodiment of *Chockmah* in the world of *Atziluth*, emanation) is YAH, spelt *Yod* + *Heh*, relating to *Sapentia*, or wisdom. This name formulates the first duality of divinity into active (*Yod*) force and passive (*Heh*) form. The extension is completed by *Binah* as the Lightning Flash of the creative process continues its expansion.

Through the *Auphanim* (*Chockmah* in the world of *Yetzirah*, formation), *Chockmah* influences the forms of all circular movements, and lays the "astral" template of swirling movements, evident in everything from the shape of shells, the physical structure of the brain and to the grand dance of planets in orbit, and the vast sprawls of spiral star-dense galaxies.

Chockmah is the first order, and that order is spiral. As Crowley drew upon the Star Atu spiral lines, quoting Zoroaster, "God is he, having the head of a hawk; having a spiral force,"[62] and as the mathematics of dynamic, non-linear systems show, "the straight line is no more than the limit of any curve."

It can be noted that the letter *Yod* is often particularly applied to *Chockmah* by many authors. *Yod* can be seen to represent the "principle" of things, and hence is suitable for *Chockmah* as representing the supreme potentiality inherent in the singularity of *Kether* but now manifesting as a swirling force.

Yod is also seen as the seed or germ, which fits with the title of *Chockmah*, AB, meaning 'father'. As *Yod* means 'hand' or 'finger', we can see in the glyph the symbol of action, direction, movement and inherently, will.

Papus describes *Yod* as the "unity-principle", and Kabbalah postulates that this principle is the source of all letters, and all

---

[62] Crowley, A. *The Book of Thoth*, p. 110.

worlds. For example, the letter *Aleph* is seen as being composed as four *Yods*, with appropriate explanation.

The *Kabbala Denudata* refers to the manipulation of *Yod* in a variety of ways, mainly in conjunction with the permutations of the divine name YHVH, but specifically states that "Yod irradiateth two", which is the numeration of *Chockmah*.

Yod has the value of ten, which is 10, and hence represents as a glyph in *Chockmah* the two proceeding stages of 1 (*Kether*) and 0 (the *Ain*). Further, it shows *Chockmah* as a source of the ten gates, and as a singularity in itself (1+0=1, which refers to the formula of 2=1, rather than that of 2=0 which *Kether* represents).

A final note can be made that the grey Hermit of the tarot can be associated with *Chockmah* as the personification of Wisdom or Moses, who spoke with God directly, and that card has the *Yod* attributed to it. The link will be further discussed in the chapter on *Chesed*. Crowley also tells of this in his esoteric fairy tale, *The Wake World*, where he says that the Hermit has "belonged to the First House from the very beginning".[63]

CHKMH totals to 73, the value of MBVKH, meaning 'Chaos', and demonstrates the stage of *Chockmah* in the cosmogenesis. The first swirlings, like the turbulent patterns in wind, water, wood and rock, are chaotic, but yet can be replicated by simple formula. The workings of *Chockmah* reveal a stochastic process, that is to say, an apparently chaotic process built on some unseen pattern and guided towards some determined goal.

The value 73 reduces to 7+3=10, again repeating the value of *Yod*, and the connection between *Kether* and *Malkuth*.

The cards to which the letters *Cheth*, *Kaph*, *Mem* and *Heh* are attributed are as follows:

---

[63] Crowley, A. 'Wake World' in *Konx om Pax*, p. 17. This piece of writing should be studied extensively and often by all practitioners of the WEIS.

Chariot

The vision of the Chariot [Ezekiel 1.1-28] deems that the "spirit of the living creature was in the wheels", and these wheels are the *Auphanim*, attributed to *Chockmah*. One of the symbols depicted on the Waite-Smith Tarot deck is that of a spinning-top, which is an appropriate demonstration of *Chockmah* (the wheel) rotating about *Kether* (the axis). The Chariot runs between *Binah* and *Geburah*, and is primarily a symbol of *Binah*, not *Chockmah*, although it bears meanings in both.

Wheel of Fortune

The Wheel of Fortune is set in motion by the extension of *Kether* into manifestation through the *Sephirah* of *Chockmah*. One meaning of this card is that of Time, but another is synchronicity, the non-causal connectiveness of things postulated by Jung in a psychoanalytical context, but a mainstay of occult teachings throughout the ages. The nature of *Chockmah* is the essence of this aspect of manifestation, in that there is no differentiation of events at this stage of the creative process.

Hanged Man

The drowned man or sacrificed God aspect of this card links with the nature of *Chockmah* as showing the sacrifice of the point of singularity by extending its essence towards manifestation. The card is also symbolic of Initiation, and hence mirrors the initiation of the creative process through *Chockmah*. In symbolic form, showing the reversal of the man, it refers to the mystic state of the Magus (the grade assigned to *Chockmah*) which is utterly opposite to the uninitiated state in that it is connected directly to the divine (Wise One of *Chockmah*) rather than the normal state of being connected to *Malkuth* (Ego state of *Yesod*).

Emperor

The Emperor has Aries assigned to it in the Zodiacal attributions, and this fits neatly with the burst of red energy of the spring equinox as a lower manifestation of the cosmic burst of creation in

Chockmah. The Emperor is the Law and the Logos as is the Magus, who gives the "Word of the Aeon".

The tarot cards in the lesser Arcana are related to each of the *Sephiroth* based on the simple principle of equal numerations. Thus, the Aces are attributed to *Kether*, the Twos to *Chockmah*, and so forth, down to the Tens which are attributed to *Malkuth*.[64] The Court Cards are attributed to the Elements, and the Major Arcana are attributed to the Paths and through them to the Zodiacal, Astrological and Elemental Systems. The suits of the cards are said to represent the worlds, or levels, at which each of the *Sephiroth* are acting. Thus, for *Chockmah* we have:

Two Wands	Dominion	Fire	Atziluth
Two Cups	Love	Water	Briah
Two Swords	Peace	Air	Yetzirah
Two Pentacles	Change	Earth	Assiah

The Two of Wands represents the energy of Fire, which is in its highest aspect as "that invisible fire that darts and flashes throughout the hidden depths of this universe" (Zoroaster). The implied dominion is that of the "pure will, unassuaged of purpose, delivered from the lust of result." (*Liber Al vel Legis*, I.44). The Magus has surrendered his Will by merging and recognising his ultimate identity as identical to that of the Universal Process.

The Two of Cups is the highest emotion of Love, that is to say, the unity of all dualities in one nature, *Chockmah*. In the world of *Briah*, Creation, Two, or duality, is the essence of that Creation.

The Two of Swords is Peace, but also it is also, according to Crowley, "silence and chastity as being the ideal purity of thought". Duality in the world of Formation signifies itself as choice, even at the level of

---

[64] For a more detailed description of the Minor cards and the Tree of Life, see Gree, A. *A Step-Up Guide to Kabbalah and Tarot.*

sub-atomic particles, where choices may take place that split an infinite number of Universes out from each point.

The Two of Pentacles is "harmonious change", which is the Tao. Crowley states that this card is a "picture of the complete manifested Universe, in respect of its dynamics". The dynamic of the Universe is Tao or Ma'at, and can be seen working at different levels through the two other *Sephiroth* of this pillar of force, *Chesed* and *Netzach*.

The colours attributed to each of the *Sephiroth* also follow a similar pattern, being divided up across the four worlds. These are known as the scales of colour, and link colour to a theory similar to sound, where notes vibrate across octaves to achieve different levels of sound. The maxim of colour, sound and number systems is that they all relate to frequencies of vibration, and the Universe is seen as a constantly active system which may be reduced to ranges of energy arrayed in levels of frequency.

King Scale: Blue - The Sky (*Masloth*).

Empress Scale: White, flecked red, blue, yellow - The robe of the justified Osiris is of these colours, which are those of the creative energy fulfilled as white.

Emperor Scale: Blue pearl grey - derived from the King and Queen scale by simple admixture.

Queen Scale: Grey - Refers to the cloudy appearance of the human seed, and the transmission of the white of *Kether* to the black of *Binah*. The colour grey is traditionally associated with age and wisdom, i.e. depictions of the Druids, Merlin, and even Gandalf "greybeard" in the fictional world of *The Lord of the Rings*.

Binah: The Angel of the Tides

A useful analogy of the creative process represented by the uppermost three *Sephiroth* of the Tree, the Supernal Triad, is that of water flowing from a tap. The source of the water is the *Kether*, whilst the pouring stream is the *Chockmah* aspect of the system. If you cup your hands into a hollow and place them in the path of the water, this represents *Binah*, the formative aspect of the creative process. The water is then formulated into tides and eddies, and moves within a defined area. The bubbles formed in this process - turbulent, chaotic and transient - are the *Da'ath*, the *non-Sephiroth* formed of the interaction between *Chockmah* and *Binah*. The water fills the well of the hands and then bursts forth between the gap of the wrists, the Abyss, and into the sink or bath as the manifestation of the lower *Sephiroth*. Thus *Binah* shapes manifestation and contains the influx of *Chockmah* and *Kether*, before transmitting the influence into manifest existence. In essence, *Binah* is manifestation itself, and thus wedded to *Malkuth*, who is sometimes seen as her daughter or a lower aspect.

Although the Supernal Triad can be seen as a cosmological model detailing the birth of the universe, it is important also to recall that the Tree is an imminent model of the current, on-going process of manifestation, and hence *Binah* is shaping reality always now, as the source of Archetypes.

Binah is the indivisible template of all things, and hence is the source of all forms, of which names are a symbolic key, and thus it is no surprise that the *Sephirah* is accorded many titles, amongst them the ultimate Mother, the primal ocean of birth, the Queen of Heaven, the bitter sea, and the city of Pyramids.

Binah is spelt in Hebrew Beth-Yod-Nun-Heh (BYNH), and is translated as 'understanding'. The word begins with *Beth*, which is taken to be the archetype of all containers, appropriate to the position of *Binah* as head of the passive pillar of form. The letters of *Binah* signify the process as follows:

Beth: The Universal Will is contained

Yod: and creates the principles of existence

Nun: passing through the fifty Gates of Understanding

Heh: into manifestation

The numbers of *Binah* are:

BYNH = 67

YHVH ALHIM = 672

TzPQIAL = 311

ShBThAI = 713

The numeration of *Binah* itself is 67, which reduces to 13, the number of Unity (*Achad*) and Love (*Abava*), the binding elements of manifestation, and further to 4, the number of manifestation. *Binah* contains 4 letters which also corresponds to its function as manifestor.

The number of the Archangel *Tzaphkiel*, relating to *Binah* in *Briah*, the world of creation, is 311, which by Gematria equates to certain relevant words:

QVRH: A beam, shelter, house (*Binah* as container)

GBVSh: Crystallisation (*Binah* as the formative process)

ShIA: Loftiness, summit, height (*Binah* as eternal rest)

Also, ShIA, 'height', can be compared with Mary, 'exalted', one of the key biblical aspects of *Binah*.

Binah interacts with *Chockmah* through the fourteenth path, to which is attributed (in the standard Golden Dawn model) to the tarot card of the Empress. The number of the card is 3, which is also the number of *Binah*, and the first of the numbers to enclose a space:

0: No space	Nought	Ain Soph Aur
1: Point	Point	Kether
2: Vector	Line	Chockmah
3: Space	Triangle	Binah

The Empress is a fitting personification of *Binah* as Mother of Life, and Nature as the formation of living things.

The tarot cards to which the letters of *Binah* are attributed are the Magician, Hermit, Death and the Emperor. These show the action of the process of *Binah*.

The Magician is the Logos, the Creative Word issued from *Chockmah* as the Universal Will, given direction and the light enclosed in a container (the light in the lamp of the Hermit). It is then transformed or translated across the Abyss (symbolised by the Death card) and the energy structured into manifestation (the Emperor bearing the "red ray" of Creation, or Aries in the Zodiacal system).

Binah, as the top of the passive pillar of Form, symbolises the ultimate feminine archetype, that of the Great Mother. The feminine can be broken down into a two-fold division, and a three-fold one:

Two-Fold System
AMA: The dark, sterile, Mother. Light Isis

AIMA: The Bright, fertile, Mother. Dark Isis

Three-Fold System
Sattva: Goodness; Maiden (First Quarter) - Mary, Isis, Nephthys

Rajas: Passion; Mother (Full Moon) - Venus, Aphrodite, Nike

Tamas: Darkness; Crone (Third Quarter) - Kalli, Lilith

Other forms of the feminine associated with *Binah* range from the *Shekinah*, the "indwelling presence of God" (also associated with *Malkuth* as the unwedded soul), to Babalon, the Great Whore or Scarlet Woman, deified by Crowley in his elaborate symbolism as the Lady Babalon, nursing the Babe of the Abyss in the City of Pyramids under the Night of Pan.

The Catholic Litany of the Blessed Virgin lists titles which could be transposed onto the Tree of Life with appropriate relevance:

Mary	i.e., exalted, also "bitterness of the sea", "Myrrh of the Sea", or "Lady/Mistress of the Sea"
Mother of Christ	*Binah* connecting to *Tiphareth*
Mother of divine grace	*Binah* connecting to *Chesed*
Mother inviolate etc	*Binah* above the Abyss of manifestation
Mirror of Justice	*Binah* connecting to *Geburah*
Seat of Wisdom	*Binah* connecting to *Chockmah*
Gate of Heaven	*Binah* as the first of the Supernals above the Abyss and connected to *Malkuth*
Refuge of Sinners	*Binah* as the place of rest
Queen of Angels	*Binah* as the *Sephirah* corresponding to the world *Briah*

The fifteen Mysteries of Mary are divided into three groups, the number of *Binah*, being the "Joyful", "Sorrowful" and "Glorious" Mysteries. The first set of five relate to the Creative and Formative (descending) aspects of *Binah*, the second set relate to the manifest aspects of *Binah*, and the third set relate to the Mystical aspects (ascending) of *Binah*.

An example is the Annunciation, which is the first "Joyful Mystery", and depicts the angel Gabriel announcing to Mary that she is to be the Mother of God. In Kabbalistic terms it can be seen that the Archangel Gabriel, attributed to *Yesod*, the "formative" aspect on a lower plane, and acts as the bearer of the "Word" or Creative Spark of *Chockmah*, the Father, into *Binah*, the Mother. Thus *Yesod* and *Binah* are linked by the attribution of Gabriel, "ruler of the waters", the waters being creation (*Binah*) and the unconscious (*Yesod*), their interface being the archetypes.

An example of the Kabbalistic interpretation of the Glorious Mysteries is that of the Assumption, where the Blessed Mother is united with her Divine Son in Heaven, which can be taken as the Mystics raising of his Awareness (*Tiphareth*, *Vau*, the Son) to transcendent universal understanding (*Binah*). Indeed, the five Glorious Mysteries can be taken as a symbolic representation of the Mystical ascent from *Tiphareth* (the first mystery of Resurrection) through the upper *Sephiroth* to *Kether* (the fifth mystery of coronation).

If *Kether* is taken to be a point, static, and *Chockmah* a line, the primary dynamic state, then *Binah* is the triangle, the first steady state of equilibrium. Indeed, *Binah* is the "Primary Definition", the original matrix of space, from which dimensions themselves spring. Thus, the quality of *Binah* in the human psyche is not the wisdom of *Chockmah*, the height of linear thinking where all implications are seen and dealt with from vast experience, but is understanding, the synthetic, connective, holistic thinking, in the form of a matrix or lattice, rather than a straight line process, which is often more direct.

In Crowley's initiatory system, the Master of the Temple (the title of the grade attributed to *Binah*) takes an oath which concludes with the intent to "interpret every phenomenon as a particular dealing of God with my soul". The understanding that all events are arising in one field of awareness is a significant attainment, although the Magus (*Chockmah*) has the further knowledge (*Da'ath*) of what the cause of that dealing is – a comprehension of the Logos.

Appropriate symbols of this state of understanding are the lattice, or net, or any object representing the concepts of linking, organisation, symmetry, and complexity.

Binah is also the *Sephirah* from which *Maya* could be seen to issue, the net of manifestation that is ultimately illusion. In the psyche, this relates to the archetypes that are hard-wired into our brain so that we perceive the universe as we do. The transcending of this biological programming is part of the Crossing of the Abyss, in a sense. We may wonder if it is indeed possible for a system to transcend itself.

Another of the concepts associated with *Binah* is faith. The idea of faith is often taken to be merely a strong belief, but true faith is more than that. As defined by Paul, faith is "the substance of things hoped for, the evidence of things not seen" [Hebrews 11.1]. Faith is that aspect of our psyche that understands aspects of the universe that cannot be translated into rational thought (i.e. *Hod*), and remain above the Abyss.

Thus, faith rests on transcendent experience, not upon belief or hope - substance and evidence must be experienced first and hence with faith "we understand [*Binah*] that the worlds were framed by the word of God [*Chockmah*], so that things which are seen were made of things which do not appear" [Hebrews 11.3].

EXERCISES

1. The Goddess is often represented as a triad of personifications; Maiden, Mother and Crone. Make a list of the characteristics of each of these three forms, and observe how closely these three categories describe the activities and behaviour of the Goddess, or Nature, or women, or the feminine aspect of men.

2. *Binah* is the *Sephirah* of form. Observe and enjoy the various ways in which humanity has created form, such as; art, architecture, dance, mathematics, music, religion and science. What is the relationship between form and meaning?

3. *Binah* can be considered as the temple; draw or sketch your ideal Temple, a place where you could work and find peace. It should also represent your understanding (the meaning of *Binah*) of the Universe; what does your idealised Temple tell you about yourself and what you want from the Universe? The Temple could be a grove of Trees, an elaborate Grecian Villa, a medieval alchemist's workshop, or even a futuristic space station. This Temple can also be used in visualisation work, dream work and ritual work.

Chesed: The Unicorn at the Waystation

Chesed, the fourth *Sephirah*, is most often translated as 'Mercy', or 'Loving Kindness'. The translations include; Mercy, grace, piety, beauty, good-will, favour, benefit, love, kindness, charity, righteousness, benevolence, to do good, to show oneself kind, to insult, reproach. In general it signifies the giving forth aspect of the Universe or the 'merciful king' aspect of God.

Whilst *Chesed* is all-giving, it is also unconstrained force and active. There is no better example of the necessity in the Tree to have balance, as *Chesed* unchecked would be all-smothering, drowning the universe in everything without form, pattern or structure. It is stupid love without sense, and on the most mundane level, it is the end of the spectrum of love which hosts stalkers and the obsessive.

If we look at *Geburah*, its opposite, we see the other far end of the scale, with controlling, destructive and manipulative aspects of love and relationship. These two have the Strength tarot card between them in the Golden Dawn model, signifying how we must constantly act to work within this spectrum of relationship.

Chesed is also called GDVLH (*Gedulah*), meaning 'greatness' or 'magnificence', and is referred to under this aspect in the line of the Lord's Prayer which states "Thou art the Power and the Glory" (*veh Gedulah, veh Geburah*). The section of the Lord's Prayer which states "Thou art the Kingdom, the Power, and the Glory" is related to the Tree of Life as follows:

Thou Art	"Ateh"	Kether
the Kingdom,	"Malkuth"	Malkuth
the Power	"veh Geburah"	Geburah
and the Glory	"veh Gedulah"	Chesed

This statement is made in the Lesser and Greater Banishing Rituals of the Pentagram which are used within esoteric ritual, with an appropriate gesture pointing to the crown of the head, below the feet, and the left and right shoulders as the Kabbalistic Cross. These rituals allow us to fully embody the Kabbalah and the Tree of Life into our experience and are not merely empty gestures and words. Rituals write into us their informing philosophy as a signature of our living relationship to the divine.

The God-name of *Chesed*, AL means "unto, towards", and again refers to the dynamic aspect of God, or the expansive force of the Cosmos. *Chesed* is the first and most active of the *Sephiroth* below the Abyss in that it is the explosion into manifestation, or *Chockmah* in a lower order.

In context of the psyche, *Chesed* is, as Dion Fortune puts it, "the formulation of the archetypal ideal, the concretion of the abstract" which forms the root of any activity.[65] Thus, the abstract principle of "settlement", Maslow's "survival motivator" is above the Abyss, but may manifest at the level of *Chesed*, and be first presented to ordinary awareness, when one is looking at purchasing a house. At the level of *Chesed*, the mind begins to formulate a sense of what the house will be when one has finished renovating it. The path connecting this formulation to awareness in *Tiphareth* is that of the Hermit, which in this sense represents the guide or way one is going to follow to achieve the realization of this formulation.

In formulating this principle, *Chesed* is reflected in *Yesod*, the foundation, by images, (*Chesed* = ChSD = 72, which can be broken down as 7 + 2 = 9, the number of *Yesod*). The images then drive our actions (*Malkuth*), powered by the dynamic desire of *Netzach*, receiving its influence direct from *Chesed* itself.

Chesed is the grand driving force of the Universe, and is often received as "love, grace or mercy in mystical experience. The experience of rapture (from the Latin, *rapere*, meaning to 'carry

---

[65] Fortune, D. *The Mystical Qabalah*, p. 163.

away') is appropriate to *Chesed*, and is again denoted by the solitary Hermit tarot card which connects *Chesed* to the *Tiphareth* (awareness) of the contemplative. Thus the myths of rape by the Gods, for example Leda and Zeus as a Swan (the bird of *Kether*) depict the various ways in which our awareness is taken away from us when we truly contact the divine, transcendent level of the Universe. The mystical passion, the height of all human devotion, is also applicable here.

Utilizing the experience of *Chesed*, the Adept is aware of the underlying, and here only just accessible, patterns and archetypes, behind the apparent world (*Malkuth*), symbols (*Yesod*) and his consciousness (*Tiphareth*). Fortune warns that functioning in *Malkuth* alone is blindness, functioning in *Yesod* alone is to be deceived by projections, and functioning in *Tiphareth* alone holds the danger of confusion of context. That is, experiences are taken as a direct dealing of God with the individual rather than as symptoms of progression to be further transcended. *Geburah* brings with it discernment so that one's own position is realized and, later, *Chesed* provides the key to the whole Psyche before the whole Psyche itself is flung into the Abyss.

The grade of *Adeptus Exemptus* is assigned to this *Sephirah*, signifying that the Adept has transcended his notion of Self as *Tiphareth* (awareness) and has moved towards the Abyss. Exempt from guilt, from sin, from all human concerns that are born of our illusionary perception of time and space, he turns to face the Great Divide. The path of the tarot card of The Wheel runs down from *Chesed*, symbolizing that the Adept at this stage has broken his illusionary attachment to apparent cause and effect, and has become the hub of the Wheel. This is a foreshadowing of the perfect state of *Chockmah*, above *Chesed*, where the Magus is simultaneously the movement of the wheel and the stillness of the hub in unbroken unity with the flow of the Universe.

Chesed is the source of magical synchronicity, and is thus an important *Sephirah* for Magicians working ritual or otherwise. It provides a means of magic more mystical than practical, the latter being the province of the *Adeptus Major* in *Geburah*.

The numerical value of *Chesed* is 4, which is the number of manifestation, and the number of the four dimensions of space and time. Thus *Chesed* is the source of time and the expansion of the Universe in time. *Chesed* is the first of the manifest *Sephiroth*, and is represented by the four-sided pyramid. This completes the sequence from the *Ain Soph Aur*: No Space (*Ain*), Point (*Kether*), Vector/Direction (*Chockmah*), Space (*Binah*), and Time (*Chesed*).

The axiom of Maria Prophetissa applies to *Chesed*, "One becomes two, two becomes three, and out of the third comes the one as the fourth". *Chesed* is the *Kether* of the Manifest, Jupiter as the Demiurge, the Gnostic creator God.

The Fours of the tarot represent the action of *Chesed* in the four worlds as follows:

Four of Wands	*Atziluth*	Perfected Work
Four of Cups	*Briah*	Lord of Pleasure
Four of Swords	*Yetzirah*	Rest from Strife
Four of Pentacles	*Assiah*	Lord of Earthly Power

The *Atziluth* of *Chesed* is the both the completion and source of all manifest power. The fire of all that may be called energy plays here, but as Crowley notes, "it is also referred to Venus in Aries, which indicates that one cannot establish one's work without tact and gentleness".[66]

At the level of *Briah*, it can be noted that the number four, the number of *Chesed*, is also a number of limitation and restriction. The equal-armed cross is not the cross of the four elements redeemed by Spirit, the fifth element, and is in some ways a full-

---

[66] Crowley, A. *Book of Thoth*, p. 190.

stop to progress in the creation process. It is only once the process continues that *Chesed* can function as a source of power.

In *Yetzirah*, the astral world, *Chesed* functions as the archetype of authority and religion, with again the danger of stagnation as dogma, convention and compromise.

In *Assiah*, *Chesed* is the establishment of the Universe in the dimensions, and the generative archetype (reflected in the procreative and generative aspects of *Netzach* at a further stage of the creative process). *Chesed* in *Assiah* signifies security, authority, and the solidity of the material plane.

The *Yetziratic* text of *Hod* states that its root is in *Chesed*, and from this, as Dion Fortune indicates, can be modelled a number of the processes of Magic. As *Chesed* is taken to be the sphere of the Secret Masters, who are taken by many magicians to guide the process of manifestation from higher planes through human adepts, it is to be approached with due consideration.

If meditation and contemplation (the stilling or focusing of the thought processes), and ritual or ceremony can be assigned to *Hod*, then through the awareness freed thereby (*Tiphareth*) we can regain *Chesed*, the grand waystation of the Universe as it pours into manifestation, and align ourselves to that flow.

A simple rite of magick involving the Egyptian Goddess Ma'at, who can be attributed to *Chesed*, designed by Maggie Ingalls demonstrates this procedure, by the meditation (*Hod*) on a flame (*Tiphareth*) and a feather (*Chesed*), which combined with a suitable Mantra links the practitioner to the Ma'at Current, which is none other than the evolutionary and stochastic current of the Universe.[67] The Hermit card also resumes this symbolism, and perhaps should be drawn bearing a quill, not a staff.

---

[67] Katz, M. *The Magister, Vol O.* pp. 105-8.

EXERCISES

1. Using a reference work on Greek legends, or Egyptian Mythology, or Celtic stories and the like, choose a God or Goddess who appeals to you. Create a representation of this deity, be it a picture, or even their name written on a sheet of paper, and place it somewhere convenient with a candle in front of it. Light the candle each morning for a few minutes, and spend that time imagining the deity. Note any synchronicities that occur with connection to the deity. Follow this exercise for a month. This is a simplified version of the devotional exercise practised by the Philosophus in Aleister Crowley's *Liber Astarte*.

3. Study the works of Jung with reference to synchronicity and archetypes. How are these processes taken into account in terms of the Tree of Life?

4. Place an object or image at each of the four quarters appropriate to each element as follows, where the elemental weapons are given as an example:

North - Earth (Pentacle)

East - Air (Sword)

South - Fire (Wand)

West - Water (Cup)

Note that the four elemental weapons are the primary tools that our species developed as extensions of our own action in the world;

Pentacle: Palm of hand for carrying objects, later a large leaf, then a flat piece of wood or stone.

Sword: Originally, the teeth for cutting and biting, then a sharp flint, and later metal edges.

Wand: First, the arm or leg, then a bone from some animal, and later a stick or wooden staff.

Chalice: The cupped hand, then a hollowed out piece of wood, and later pottery and metal cups.

Geburah: The Folding of the Robe

Geburah is the fifth *Sephirah* of the creative process, and signifies in Hebrew a number of related meanings around the theme of strength:

> **Geburah**: Strength, power, force, valour, courage, victory, might, God, strong, mighty, hero.

Geburah is connected with the punishment of God, rigor, severity, and justice. An alternative title of this *Sephirah* is *Pachad*, meaning 'fear'. Its most negative aspect is said to be blind fanaticism, which is often the result of a fear of that which is considered different to one's own beliefs. When the seven sins are allocated to the Tree, the sin of *Geburah* is said to be that of anger. It is also connected, in a more positive sense, with discipline and energy. Obviously, these aspects are counter-balanced by those of *Chesed*, 'loving kindness' or 'mercy', on the opposite side of the Tree, across the path marked by the Strength card of the tarot. That card can be taken to depict the harmonized relationship between *Geburah*, symbolized by the Red Lion, and *Chesed*, symbolized by the Peaceful Lady, whose own demeanour in sufficient to placate the beast.

It should be noted that *Geburah* is passive to *Chesed*, and that as Dion Fortune states, many of the social and psychological problems we face can be modelled by our constant functioning, inappropriately, with an active *Geburah*. That is to say, we shoot first and ask questions later, or allow our fear to drive us rather than our urges to creativity. If *Chesed* were not constrained by a correctly functioning *Geburah*, life would become dysfunctional in the opposite extreme, with chaos and anarchy without point. It is the work of the Adept grades in the initiatory system to learn to balance these states both within and without, to ensure that *Tiphareth*, the pivotal point of the Tree, is maintained in a dynamic equilibrium.

The *Zohar* puts it that the "left arm draws the immensity of space in rigor", and that *Geburah* is associated with the "repentance of God" and the Archangel Samael. It also points out that Mercy and Severity are united in *Tiphareth*.

The *Sepher Yetzirah* states "the fifth path is called the Radical Intelligence, because it is more similar than any other to the Supreme Unity and emanates from the depths of the Primordial Wisdom." It is the conciliatory force, restricting and directing the expansion of *Chesed*. The link with *Kether* is in its role in defining the process of *Zimzum* as *Din*, which will be examined later in this chapter. The connection to "primordial wisdom", or *Chockmah* represents that *Geburah* plays a role in connection with the expansion of *Chesed* (the "*Chockmah* below the Abyss", as explained in the former chapter) in a similar way to the role played by *Chockmah* in ordering the first swirling resulting from the expansion of *Kether*.

Indeed, it is hard to examine *Geburah* without connecting it with *Chesed*, or showing how the two merge into *Tiphareth* as a functional Triad. *Geburah*, like all the *Sephiroth* is only one snapshot of a synergetic process, or one node of a network, and thus can only be fully expressed as a relationship to the whole.

If *Chesed* is the irrepressibly expanding impulse of love and growth, then *Geburah* is the counteracting restraint and concentration. If *Chesed* is the inclination towards things, the outgoing nature and the opening-up of the psyche, then *Geburah* is the inward withdrawal of powers and the concentration of power. In *Tiphareth* is married these dynamic attributes of attraction and repulsion.

An example of the difference between the two *Sephiroth* is further provided in the martial arts, and can be found in any other system, where the flow of *Tai Chi Chuan* is that akin to *Chesed*, whereas the *Chi* focusing of *Kung Fu* is of the nature of *Geburah*.

Din, or 'judgment', associated with *Geburah*, plays an important role in the doctrine of *Zimzum*, "contraction", detailing the creative process of manifestation. In this Lurianic doctrine, *Ain Soph* gathered the roots of Din and placed them aside for the process of *Zimzum*, thus showing the withdrawal of the point of *Kether* from the *Ain Soph Aur* as a concentrated act of judgement and self-limitation. Indeed, it could be called the "original definition", and *Geburah* embodies the qualities of definition in its aspect as positive limitation.

In cosmological terms, *Geburah* represents the state 300,000 years after the Point Zero of the Big Bang model, the "Epoch of Recombination" (at -255 degrees), where heavy chemical elements were first formed in the gravitational collapse of stars and the first formation of galaxies. In Kabbalistic terminology, "the Left hand of God traced the firmament". In the *Book of the Law*, by Aleister Crowley, a similar model is utilized in symbolism:

> III.72. I am the Lord of the Double Wand of Power; the wand of the force of Coph Nia - but my left hand is empty, for I have crushed an Universe; & naught remains.

The *Zohar* describes this development in terms of *malbush*, a 'garment', whose folds create the matrix of manifestation as the letters of the Hebrew alphabet recombine as the folds overlap. This mirrors modern cosmology, as it is stated in Kabbalah that an "unmatched Yod" remains once the combinations have taken place, which then transmits the light of *Ain Soph Aur* into the creative process and manifestation (signified by the Hermit tarot card).

This is similar to chemistry and physics, where unmatched particles form the basis of further reactions and energy bounds. Indeed, the recent discovery of background radiation from the edge of the cosmos is written in identical terms, as the Epoch of recombination, the first ripples of cosmic structure, and is the stage where light was set free from the foggy soup of radiation.

Dion Fortune writes that "*Binah* is perpetually binding force into form, and *Geburah* perpetually breaking up and destroying all forms" via the preserving influence of *Chesed*.[68]

The *Sepher ha-Temunah*, amongst other works, uses the doctrine of cosmic cycles associated with the *Sephiroth*. These cycles or the *shemittah*, are said to last 6000 years, and are associated with the seven *Sephiroth* below the Abyss, thus making 42,000 years (or 49,000 years if the cycle is 7000 years), leaving the last 8000 or 1000 years to complete the "Great Jubilee", (the Jubilee is a period of 50 years). It is said that we are currently in the *Shemittah* of Judgement, presided over by *Geburah*, which matches the Thelemic "Aeon of Horus" and the "Kali Yuga" of the Hindu system.

If this system is applied to the big bang cosmological model, then it is apparent that we had exactly 50 cycles to reach the Epoch of Recombination, the first Cosmic Jubilee, and that cycle would have been that of *Malkuth*, or manifestation.

The process of *Gematria* may be applied in a number of ways to this *Sephirah*, as follows:

Geburah is spelt GBVRH, numerating to 216, which is also the value of DBIR (Holy of Holies, Inner Sanctuary), and ChVBR (Sorcerer, snake-charmer). This latter value reminds us that *Geburah* functions as the restrictive influence on the process of the Tree, whether that of the lightning flash of creation down the Tree, or the Snake of evolution up the Tree. We can extend that metaphor by suggesting a snake uses fear, *Geburah*, to freeze its victims and that the vibrations caused by a snake-charmers pipe act as a *Chesed* on the serpent of fear that is *Geburah*. When we see these processes around us every day in our world, we come soon to appreciate their power in modelling all aspects of our existence, from the marketplaces of Marrakesh to the inner sanctuary of our soul.

The value of *Geburah*, 216, is also the value of RAIH (Proof, evidence). Whilst not an immediately obvious correspondence, we might apply this word to the grade of the *Sephirah*, as in the initiatory process up the Tree, it is where the *Adeptus Major* attains a complete mastery of practical magic. This is the final evidence and

---

[68] Fortune, D. *The Mystical Qabalah*, p. 183.

proof of the initiatory system itself and all matters related to it. Another twist of our numerology reveals that 216 = 6 x 6 x 6, the number of man given in Revelations.

We can go much further when we begin to use *Gematria*, to make a vast web of correspondences across systems. We can take the corresponding Hebrew God-name of the *Sephirah* which is ALHIM GBVR, the God of Judgement. This name has the value of 57, as does the word NVAP (Satyr). The Greek god Pan, lord of satyrs, can be associated with *Geburah* in his aspect of panic and awe, when *Geburah* is also called *Pachad*, meaning 'fear'.

We can then look at the Archangel of the *Sephirah*, Kamiel, equating as KMAL to 91, which is the same value as AMN (Amen), LBNH (Moon), MLAKh (messenger), PHOD (robe), MAN (to refuse), and EHLON (Tree). These corresponding words can lead to more contemplation on the nature of *Geburah* and its divine role in our life.

If we feel that these correspondences are a stretch too far, we can at least now properly read the secret and sacred texts of authors such as Aleister Crowley. Buried in virtually every sentence is Kabbalah and numerology, through this use of correspondences. In *The Daughter of the Horseleech*, writing of the very God-name and Archangel we have just listed, *Elohim Gibor* and *Kamael* Crowley writes, "He too bore the wings and weapons of space and Justice, and in himself he was that great Amen that is the beginning and end of all." It is evident that Crowley was referring to the correspondence of the number 91 between Kamiel and Amen, and not just simply being poetic.

A brief digression can be made at this point to mention one of the over-utilisations of Gematria. As a system of numerology, Gematria is useful in that many Kabbalists used it simply as a form of code, as did Crowley. That there is a belief that each letter/number embodies a unique essence, and that these can be equated with one another can be looked at as either real, or simply a useful form of thought-provoking letter play. However, one cannot take the belief, and then in other cases step outside of the structure that the belief has meaning within. The Golden Dawn society referred to this as one example of a "confusion of the hierarchies".

Other examples are common in some New Age writings where beliefs are taken out of context of the systems which make sense of them - one that springs to mind is that of *Karma*.

The Planet of *Geburah* is Mars, MDIM, equalling 654, as do LHTIM (Secret arts, enthusiasm and witchcraft) and DMDVM (Twilight, dim light). This again suggests the mastery of practical magic as the skill attained in the initiatory system. The twilight follows the Day of *Tiphareth* and precedes the Night of the Abyss during the ascent of the Tree.

The Gods associated with *Geburah* are those of a martial nature, such as Thor, Ares, Mars, Horus, and Montu. Obviously, warfare and revenge are amongst the attributes given to such deities, but one should also see that *Geburah* embodies strict rulership and kingly attributes as well. Despite their superficiality, the *Conan* adventure stories of Robert E. Howard depict the translation of the barbarian aspects of *Geburah* into those required by the just king of a realm (learning when to hold one's tongue as effective diplomacy rather than lash out in anger is a lesson learnt from *Geburah*).

The Weapons of the *Sephirah* are the sword, scourge and spear. In *Magick*, Crowley replaces the Spear with the dagger, and states that the weapons symbolise the following essential qualities in the Magicians world:

SCOURGE	DAGGER	CHAIN
Sulphur	Mercury	Salt
Energy	Fluidity	Fixity
Pain	Death	Bondage

The Scourge keeps the Aspiration keen, the Dagger shows that the magician is determined to make any Sacrifice required, and the Chain restricts his Wandering. The three binding items surround the Holy Oil, representing consecration, Grace and aspiration. This could be taken to symbolise in the concentric circles model of Kabbalah that *Geburah* is the outer circle of *Chesed*, which has its roots in *Binah*, to which the Oil can be associated.

Wippler notes that one can meditate on *Geburah* and *Chesed* as analysis and synthesis, in order to reach an accurate self-evaluation.[69] This resumes the idea of the tarot card Justice, on the Path running from *Geburah* to *Tiphareth*, the central *Sephirah* of balance. A useful object of meditation for this Triad, and indeed any part of the Tree would be a Prism, into which light enters as a single ray, and emerges split into the visible spectrum of colours. This signifies the process of manifestation down the Tree, as the Unified State is manifest in apparently separate states, objects and identities.

On the psychological level, *Geburah* represents the Super-Ego, with its nature of punishment, whilst *Chesed* represents the Ego-Ideal, with its reward functioning when the Self in *Tiphareth* meets this Ideal. These all function pre-self, and are thus in the individual unconscious. As the processes of *Chesed* and *Geburah* take place before awareness (*Tiphareth*), one cannot deal with them directly. Rather, one must observe their manifestation in awareness (*Tiphareth*), and trace back one's emotions, thoughts, beliefs and actions (*Netzach*, *Hod*, *Yesod* and *Malkuth*) to their source.

Halevi, based on the work of Freud in particular, notes that the source of this conscience is originally formed from the parental model, and thus must be observed, and replaced by an individualised conscience. This is one of the minor inversions of work defined by the Tree as the Initiate progresses. It is interesting to note that when the Ten Commandments are allocated to the Tree, that of *Geburah* is "honour thy father and mother". We can suggest that this is Kabbalistically interpreted as recognising the

---

[69] González-Wippler, M. *A Kabbalah for the Modern World*, pp. 186-7.

elements of parental conditioning in one's own nature and by analysis and synthesis, observing in awareness, judge which are appropriate, and which are not, discarding the latter and forming one's own model.

We must note that the punishment/reward complex signified by these two *Sephiroth* is a simplistic and dangerous model, as punishment, whether inflicted from without or within, only changes behaviour and not cause. Working for reward, again whether self-reward or peer-reward goes against the dictum of working "without lust of result" which is central to success. As already noted, the "trick" of working the two *Sephiroth* is, as one should expect from the system, pictured on the tarot card connecting the two, which is Strength. The woman (Mercy) rests her hand upon the head of the lion (Severity) without conflict. The Key represents an act of *Tikkun*, restoration and reintegration, or restoring elements to their appropriate role in the creative process.

Sturzaker states that *Geburah* is the "centre of the dark night of the soul", which relates to the progress between *Tiphareth* and *Binah*, and the Crossing of the Abyss.[70]

Dion Fortune terms the *Sephirah* as the "sacrificial Priest of the Mysteries", and resumes a description of *Geburah* as involved with the transmutation of force from one level to another (i.e. sacrificing coal in a furnace to turn into steam and drive the engine).[71] This is the true nature of sacrifice as represented by *Geburah*, rather than that of *Tiphareth*, which is a sacrifice based on an incorrect belief that is not shed until after the awareness appropriate to *Tiphareth* is attained. Even at the stage of *Geburah*, an incomplete understanding is reached, although as Crowley states, the Moral is "Become an Adeptus Major!", if one wants to "easily understand how to perform them [operations of Magick art] if necessary".[72]

---

[70] Sturzaker, J. *Kabbalistic Aphorisms*, p. 23
[71] Fortune, D. *The Mystical Qabalah*, p. 176.
[72] Crowley, A. *Magick*, p. 299.

Fortune also points out the connection of *Chesed* and *Geburah* with running a group, or managing a team. She symbolises it by making an analogy to the reins of a horse team, where sometimes one needs to let the rein out, and sometimes one needs to rein the horse in sharply. This is part of the Mystery of the Chariot, the tarot card running from *Binah* (Understanding) to *Geburah* (Severity). In modern management training, a balanced *Geburah* is the difference between aggressiveness and assertiveness.

The Paths of Rigour which lead to and from *Geburah* can be categorised as follows:

Cheth – Chariot: The Mystery of Directing

Teth - Strength: The Mystery of Control

Lamed – Justice: The Mystery of Equilibrium

Mem - Hanged Man: The Mystery of Sacrifice

It should be noted that *Geburah* ultimately is only destructive to the transitory. If something is "real", no amount of doubt, analysis, examination, and so forth will destroy it. Thus the principle of Occam's Razor (the simplest explanation will suffice in cases of doubt) is a sound one. A final note comes from the *Thirteen Petalled Rose*, where an analysis of the *Kiddush* ritual (that performed on the eve of the Sabbath), states that the cup signifying reception contains red wine, expressing an aspect of *Geburah*, but has a small amount of water added to represent the mercy of *Chesed*.[73] It is important in all acts to harmonise *Geburah* and *Chesed* in *Tiphareth* to achieve equilibrium, as will be examined in the following Chapter.

EXERCISES

1. Take a picture, a favourite painting or photograph, or a tarot card, and make a list of as many separate objects, colours and

---

[73] Steinsaltz, A. *The Thirteen Petalled Rose*, p. 179.

images on it as you can. This illustrates the process of discernment, and definition, which is the process of separation. Think of appropriate and inappropriate ways that this process is utilised by yourself in your daily life.

2. Find common examples of sacrifice, in terms of the transmutation from one form to another. Observe the role sacrifice plays in nature, and its necessity. What are the usual barriers to sacrifice?

3. Find an example where control is seen to be exercised. What is control, and how does it work? What is its counterbalance? What assumptions about the Universe does 'control' rely on, and how true is it that anything can be "controlled"?

Tiphareth: The Hub of Sacrifice

The text of the *Sepher Yetzirah* regards *Tiphareth* as a "mediating intelligence" which multiplies the flow of emanations into it, and communicates these emanations to those who unite with it. We see that *Tiphareth* is placed in the centre of the Tree in most versions of the diagram, acting as a busy crossroads for the operations of the *Sephiroth* above it and below it.

When someone is absolutely central to operations, when you feel at the centre of a situation, when everything is revolving around you or something else, then that (or you) has become a *Tiphareth*. In our Solar System, the Sun is our centre, and so it is no surprise that the Sun corresponds to *Tiphareth*, as does the Self, and Christ or other saviour Gods of various religions.

As a mediator (from the Latin, meaning "middle"), *Tiphareth* can function as a translator and diplomat, organising the activities of the Upper and Lower Tree according to the dual states of each. This is the point where "as is below, so above" is equally "as is above, so below". The Upper *Sephiroth* cannot flow into the Lower in an optimum state if the Lower are unbalanced, and neither can the Lower *Sephiroth* function correctly when the upper *Sephiroth* are disturbed.

Tiphareth, the *Sephirah* representing human self-awareness, is the key-stone on which this balance rests. In Ephesians 2.20, Paul makes reference to "the foundation of the apostles and prophets, Jesus Christ himself being the chief corner-stone," which from a Kabbalistic point of view can be read to say that *Yesod* ('foundation') is the *Sephirah* of prophecy and communication to the outside world (*Malkuth*), but the corner-stone of that process is the self-awareness as practised by Christ, a personification of *Tiphareth*.[74]

---

[74] See *Imitation of Christ*, Thomas à Kempis, p. 74, "It is the mark of a perfect man, Lord, never to let his mind relax in attention to heavenly things, and to pass

Equally, the role of a mediator is often that of translation, and it is in translation we find *Tiphareth* functioning as the *Sephirah* of sacrifice, the translation of one state to another by release of the old pattern. An example is the sacrificial flame, where the wick (matter) is translated by fire (spiritual practice) into light (illumination). Thus, the ever-burning lamp is a reminder of this task, as well as symbolising the ultimate goal of the *Ain Soph Aur* as explained in the chapter, 'Crown of Tsimtsum', previously.

In the WEIS, the Adeptus Minor, the Grade attributed to *Tiphareth*, finds themselves of necessity abandoning old patterns of belief and behaviour based on previous (*Yesod*-dominated) views of the world and their relationship to it, in favour of new goals responding to unification with *Tiphareth* and the influences now being felt for the first time in actuality from the upper *Sephiroth*. The difference in their behaviour is notable, as up until that state, "we see through a glass, darkly" (I.Cor.13:12).

Tiphareth, as with each of the *Sephiroth*, requires examination as part of a set of complex processes. The paths connected to *Tiphareth* give aspects of its relationships to the other *Sephiroth* of the Tree. It is important to note firstly, though, that there is only one *Sephiroth* to which *Tiphareth* does not directly connect, and that is *Malkuth*. Our awareness of our environment is always seen through *Yesod*, the "dark glass" of our own perspective, beliefs and senses.

We will look at how these paths shed light on our heart, a primary correspondence of *Tiphareth*, through the tarot cards that illustrate these paths connecting *Tiphareth* to the other *Sephiroth*. We will use the Golden Dawn system of correspondences for this analysis, which can also be conducted with other systems such as the Waite-Trinick. We can also look at these paths in three distinct groups, based on their positions relative to *Tiphareth* on the Tree, which

---

through many cares as though he had none; not as an indolent man does, but by having the certain prerogative of a free mind no disorderly affection for any created being".

helps us group the tarot cards together into smaller groups for comparison and contrast.

The Paths Of the Heart

A. The God of the Heart

II. **High Priestess:** This path connects *Tiphareth* to *Kether* and is the path of transcendence from self-identification to universal-identification. It functions as the impact of our true state into our self-aware state (when operating as awakened consciousness by various practices), and hence the High Priestess shows *Tiphareth* as a measure of our reflection of Truth, which hence flows into the Lower *Sephiroth*.

IV. **Emperor:** The Emperor represents the Power accessible to the fully operating *Tiphareth* from *Chockmah*, the Source of all movement and direction. The Emperor is the Light of Creation which bears one upwards through the letter *Heh*, meaning 'window'.

VI. **Lovers:** Operating at the same level as the Emperor, but on the other side of the Tree, the Lovers represent the impact of inspiration from *Binah*, 'Understanding'. Regardie also notes that one interpretation of the card is "the liberating effect of the descent of the Higher Genius", a specific experience attributed to *Tiphareth*.

B. The Initiation of the Heart

IX. **Hermit:** The Hermit connects Awareness to the expansive force of *Chesed*, 'Loving kindness' or 'Mercy'. The Hermit embodies the contemplation of the Heart on the Mysteries of Creation in the Inner silence of devotion. As the Sufi saying states, "The Worker is hidden in the Workshop".

XI. **Justice:** The Atu of Justice is the balance of *Tiphareth* with respect to *Geburah*, discrimination. *Lamed*, the letter attributed to the Path, is the 'ox goad', and symbolises the work of the Initiate in balancing the "two cells" which St. Catherine of Siena speaks of, where "...if you dwelt in self-knowledge alone, you would despair; if you dwelt in the knowledge of God alone, you would be tempted to presumption. One must go with the other, and thus you will reach perfection."

C. The Trials of the Heart

XIII. **Death**: Passing through the Veil of *Paroketh*, the Path to which the Death Atu corresponds, connects to *Netzach*, one of the *Sephiroth* involved with the active creation of Life. This juxtaposition points to the awareness that Life and Death are not opposites, but phases in the same process. Although even this duality may be found in later states as false, it is an important recognition and one essential to the understanding of sacrifice.

XIV. **Temperance**: The Temperance card symbolises the state when *Tiphareth* is functioning to harmonise the Lower *Sephiroth*, whereas the High Priestess, its equivalent on the Middle Pillar above the Veil, shows the effects on *Tiphareth* of the proper functioning of the Upper *Sephiroth*. The Golden Dawn rituals of advancement to the state of *Tiphareth* and the grade of Adeptus Minor always move the candidate along one side path, then bar them, then move along the opposite path to be barred and forced to return, until at last the "Middle Way" is walked and the goal attained.

XV. **Devil**: The Devil Atu, partnering Death on the other side of the Tree, shows how *Hod*, the Intellect, can enslave the Awareness by being glorified for its own sake. There are many paradoxes which can break the chains of the Devil, and Zen *Koans* are specifically designed to work on this level, amongst others. It also shows the danger of attempting to make *Netzach* subservient to *Hod* (working on 'controlling the emotions') and is a parody of the more appropriate discipline which can be entered into by balancing the Square Dance of *Geburah* and *Chesed* with *Hod* and *Netzach* in *Tiphareth*.

Having looked at the *Sephirah* in general and the connecting paths, we will conclude by touching upon how concepts bound up with

Tiphareth were used in ritual by the Golden Dawn, and how that works through correspondence.

The Lines of Sacrifice

In *777*, a dictionary of correspondences, numerology and Kabbalah, Crowley attributes three "Magical Formula" to *Tiphareth*, these being ABRAHADABRA, IAO and INRI. These "formula" are sequences of letters or concepts, bound by correspondence and expanded into philosophies or practice. The creation and elucidation of such formula is one of many magical practices in itself within the WEIS and drawing from such practices as Kabbalistic permutation.

The latter two are expounded by Regardie in *Foundations of Practical Magic*, but bear some brief mention here as examples of how we can learn from such formula, which may appear esoteric and unnecessarily complex at first sight, but reveal nuanced models of reality that are just as difficult to convey in any other language. We may have to crack the code to comprehend them, but when we do, we may also come to a new consciousness of the world.

IAO is a formula created from the first letters of three ancient Egyptian deities; Isis, Apophis and Osiris. It can be summarised as the formula describing three phases in all systems, be they events, acts or psychological occurrences. The formula describes the three phases as Growth (Isis), Death (Apophis) and Rebirth (Osiris). As an example, the dynamics of a Facebook group goes through these phases, as do ones personal resolutions, or even a day at work. When we are aware of these phases, we can recognise and welcome the Apophis phase as a necessary evil, and work better to time the Osiris phase as appropriate to a situation.

In further playing with correspondence, Crowley connects the IAO formula by the Gematria of 17 (the letters add as 10 + 1 + 6) to the numbers of squares of the Flyflot Cross and from that to the Aleph which shares the same shape as that cross, and from the Aleph to the concept of unity, as Aleph = 1. This suggests that the IAO formula signifies the unity of all activity broken into three stages of motion, although we take several steps of correspondence to get that conclusion.

We can also look at the corresponding tarot cards for illustration of this formula, and for use in ritual or meditation. In this case we have the Hermit, Fool and Sun. We do not have a direct correspondence for the letter "O" as Hebrew has no vowels, but we can use the direct correspondence of Osiris to the daily death and rebirth of the Sun.

If we were to imagine a reading where we received those three cards, it would possibly suggest to us that all growth and success (Sun) comes from letting go and being free (Fool) so that our true path (Hermit) may have space to be discovered through all its trials. We can also contemplate the symbolism of the Fool and the Hermit being atop the mountain, with the Sun above. These contemplations activate the formula in our awareness, and lead to new ways of experiencing the world, and more importantly, new behaviours and decisions; it is magic to engage life, not escape it.

INRI is taken as a shorthand version of various phrases, but the most usual is the Latin for "Jesus of Nazareth, King of the Jews". In the version of Kabbalah developed by the Golden Dawn this phrase embodies the mystery of *Tiphareth* in its analysis as the Hebrew letters of Yod, Nun, Resh and Yod. We take the letters as the first letters of ancient Egyptian deities as before, and make a further correspondence to their zodiacal, elemental or planetary symbol.

I	Virgo	ISIS
N	Scorpio	APOPHIS
R	Sun	OSIRIS
I	Virgo	ISIS

A few Golden Dawn rituals have the practitioner actually create various letters from the position of their arms to fully embody the formula being utilised. If we take another formula such as the letters LVX, meaning 'light', we create those letters as an "L" representing the 'mourning of Isis' (we lean our head upon the outstretched arm, with our other arm slightly bent but upright, like a dancer signifying mourning), a "V" for Apophis (making a 'Victory' type 'V' with our arms) and an "X" on our breast with our arms crossed (for the rising of Osiris, and of course, the cross of Christ).

In fact, in an unpublished Golden Dawn manuscript (see the MAGISTER Vol. 0) these positions of the body were even further mapped out in a form of cosmic-correspondence-yoga to a seasonal clock-face and the transitions of the equinox and solstices as the light and darkness changes through the year. As we make a "V" sign with our arms, we only encompass a small bit of light, as the rest of our clock-face is full of the darkness, so Apophis is briefly triumphant, for example. It may be a case of a correspondence too far, and perhaps why it was never included in the "Complete" Golden Dawn materials – which are far from complete – but for some, it might open their mind to vast cosmological cycles even in the most simple of physical actions; a thoroughly western Yoga.

As with the *Tetragrammaton* of YHVH, this INRI formula repeats a key letter at the start and end of the formula to indicate that events have a natural cycle. In this case, we are going through growth, death, rebirth and growth again. When we consider the four worlds model, and *Tiphareth* as the heart from which each higher Tree emerges, we might be reminded of this spiral and dynamic model which speaks of a never-ending evolution through increasingly rarefied planes.

EXERCISES

1. Attempt to translate a phrase or sentence from another language such as Hebrew or Latin, word by word using an appropriate dictionary; note the difficulties in arriving at a singular meaning for the message by taking this approach. In a similar fashion, this demonstrates how *Tiphareth* is the overall comprehension that follows from the piece by piece process of *Geburah*.

2. Observe a group of people or other social system, and discover who or what is functioning as the *Tiphareth* centre of the group. Note how much the social order and the actions of the group revolve from the *Tiphareth* location. Where does the *Tiphareth* individual get his inspiration from in order to influence the group?

3. Collect images of the Heart from any sources you have available to you. The religious systems of Ancient Egypt and Medieval Christianity provide useful sources, as do the Ancient Mexican religions of the Toltecs and Mayans. What does the heart symbolise?

Netzach: The Rose in the Lamplight

The *Sepher Yetzirah* deems *Netzach*, "the Hidden Intelligence, for it pours forth a brilliant splendour onto all intellectual virtues which are looked upon with the eyes of the spirit and the ecstasy of faith." In most readings of the Tree as a model of the human being, *Netzach* is described as the seat of the emotions, partnering *Hod*, the seat of the Intellect.

As the base of the positive pillar, and as the first of the *Sephiroth* in the creative process below the veil of *Paroketh*, *Netzach* functions as nature's dynamo, storing and transmitting the explosion of *Chockmah* sent to it from *Chesed*, the *Sephirah* of expansion. As *Chesed* is the *Chockmah* below the Abyss, so *Netzach* is the *Chockmah* below the Veil. We may see this as a constant stepping down of the original essence of creation through a transformer system.

On a psychological level, the Tree indicates that *Netzach* is active in respect of *Hod*, and *Hod* passive to the influence of *Netzach*. This symbolises that our inner state should be one where our emotions are allowed creative expression, through our thoughts (*Hod*), imagination (*Yesod*) and actions (*Malkuth*). A startling scientific experiment has shown that such is the case, whether we choose to believe it or not. Our conscious registration of an inner decision occurs after the brain has already set that action in process, demonstrating that conscious free will is but a convenient fiction. We are all living milliseconds in the past, removed by our own neurology from the events taking place in the environment and the acts performed by ourselves.[75]

The work of *Netzach* undertaken by the Initiate serves to continue these themes. As the central core of selfhood is approached in *Tiphareth*, it is increasingly obvious that a grand synthesis needs to take place. Thus, the work of *Netzach* involves both the practice of

---

[75] See Libet, B. *Mind Time*.

Dharana, which seeks to unite the awareness with the object of which it is aware, by concentration, contemplation, or meditation, and the practice of *Bhakti Yoga*, which is the union with deity through the practice of devotion.

As Seven, the number of *Netzach*, is often taken to be the number of completion, we can see that as the Initiate rises to this *Sephirah*, he completes equally at one level the work of the Lower *Sephiroth*. Indeed, the Golden Dawn stated that the advancement through the Elemental Initiations of the Lower *Sephiroth* "in a sense, quitteth not *Malkuth*".

That is to say, partly, that the work of those Grades is aligned to ones outside observations, even when directed at the Psyche, whereas the Work beyond that point has undergone the Holy Inversion and is involved with the Upper *Sephiroth* and the experiences and states that transcend the personality construct.

Further, the Rose (taken as a symbol of *Tiphareth*) and the Lamp (a symbol of *Kether* and the *Ain Soph Aur*) are both attributed to *Netzach*, which may reflect its sevenfold nature of completion. The seven-petalled rose alludes to the sevenfold pattern, and was used by Bosch as emblem DCCXXIII of the *Ars Symbolica*, and by Fludd in the *Summum Bonum*. It is to this Rose of Completion that the Golden Dawn aim in their elemental initiations, as a pre-shadowing of the Rose-Cross of *Tiphareth* and the Rose of Light in *Kether*.

Charles Harness uses this symbolism in his magnificent short story, *The Rose*, where the next stage of human progression is embedded in the ballet of the "Nightingale and the Rose". In the original story of Oscar Wilde's from which this fictional ballet is based, the nightingale sacrifices itself on a white rose in order to make it red. This could be read as the sacrifice of *Netzach*, where sensual passion is transfused into mystical passion through the path of Death, the tarot Atu placed on the path uniting *Netzach* and *Tiphareth*.

One other aspect of *Netzach* expressed in the psyche is that of the instinctual construct. This construct can be broken into a number of circuits; Bio-Survival, Emotional-Territorial, Semantic and Socio-Sexual. These function largely unconsciously in the undeveloped, *Yesod*-dominated, persona, and are usually examined in the early stages of the Initiate's development. Obviously, many of the functions of these mechanisms are not designed to be consciously controlled, for example, the beating of the heart or the reflexive action of the muscles. The fight, freeze or flee instinct also takes place in *Netzach*. Thus, one can be running away from danger before one has time to think about it, which is when the impulse reaches *Hod* a moment later.

These instincts run straight into the World of Action simultaneously with their transmission to the process of thought, and this is modelled by Kabbalah on the path leading from *Netzach* to *Hod*. The tarot Atu symbolising this path is that of the Moon, Mistress of Mystery and the emotional, shadowy side of the psyche. The Moon also governs the cyclic aspects of nature, as well as the tides and feminine menstrual energies. It is therefore appropriate that the letter attributed to this path is that of *Qoph*, meaning 'back of the head', where the more primitive parts of the brain reside, regulating these energies.

Netzach is spelt in Hebrew, NTzCh, *Nun-Tzaddi-Cheth*. The tarot attributions of these cards are Death, the Star, and the Chariot. The corresponding ancient Egyptian deities of this sequence are revealing of *Netzach*, being Typhon, Nuit and Hormakhu:

> **Typhon** (or Seth) is the serpent deity connected with storms, natural phenomena appropriate to *Netzach*, and was the pilot of the solar boat (*Tiphareth*) who speared Apophis, symbolic of the Death Atu connecting *Netzach* to *Tiphareth*.

> **Nuit** resided in the "lower mansion of Heliopolis", which is the house of the sun, and again refers to *Netzach*'s relationship to *Tiphareth*, to which the Sun is ascribed. She also was responsible for keeping the forces of Chaos

breaking through into the world, which denotes *Netzach* function in maintaining regularity to the expansions of *Chesed*.

Harmachis is Horus of the Horizon, and is connected with the Sphinx, which in turn is symbolic of the four elemental *Sephiroth*. The horizon is that of the Veil of Paroketh.

The *Sephirah* embodies the energies of transmutation through Sacrifice, Hope and Rebirth.

EXERCISES

1. Make a study of the relationship between Religion and Love. The raptures of Christian mystics, the experiences and stories told by the Sufi schools, and the devotional work of Magicians such as Aleister Crowley will provide numerous examples of how love can be seen as both a result and a method of mystical experience.

2. Take a number of actions and observe which emotion, or complex of emotions, is driving the action. What is the relationship between emotion, thought and deed, and how does Kabbalah model this?

3. Observe your own devotional activities and bring them into your whole work; moments when you lose yourself, such as in dance, drinking, watching a sunset, or making love. What do these experiences tell us about the relationship between self-awareness and activity?

4. Wherever you find yourself alone or with a group and with twenty minutes or so to spare, collect together ten small objects you can find in your vicinity and lay them out in a Tree of Life pattern. The ten objects must correspond to the ten *Sephiroth*.

So for example, you might find a white circle of paper that has been punched out of a piece of paper for a ring-binder. This would make an ideal *Kether*, even more so that it was punched out of something that is no longer apparent. A lost pencil on the floor could make a

Chockmah, showing how the point of *Kether* extends into a line. It would also have a clever reference to the drawing of the sacred letters when they are described as "black fire on white". A paperback book with a Sun on the cover would make a *Tiphareth*, and so forth. This is how the exercise would work in a library on a rainy day.

The first time we played this exercise we were on a picnic in a group by the riverside and had a group of children go looking for objects. They were told what sort of objects we were looking for and received a semi-Kabbalistic education that day out as well as being kept out of our way for an hour.

We eventually ended up with nine objects other than our *Netzach*. The group leader called everyone back and we were wondering what we could go look for that would be special and other than "something natural" which was everywhere. Suddenly we all looked up across from us and there was a deer standing looking at us, stood underneath a tree, pawing its hoof at the ground. A shaft of sunlight broke through the cloud and illuminated it, just so we were sure this was something divine.

As we looked, it appeared to nod, then turned and ran off. We all went to the base of the Tree and the hoof had upturned the most perfect circular green mossy-covered stone – our *Netzach*.

Hod: The Crystal Watercourse

In the psyche, *Hod* is the intellect as balanced against the *Sephirah* of the emotions, *Netzach*. The Alchemical Hermaphrodite is composed of these two *Sephiroth*, as Hermes represents the Mind, and Aphrodite the Emotions. Thus *Hod* is specifically the power of the mind, the thoughts and the mental will. It acts as a lower arc of *Chockmah*, the Divine Will, and a lower level of *Geburah*, discrimination, and *Binah*, understanding. All these are reflected in the process of thought, as we structuralise our perceptions of the environment and our intuitive processes.

In a way, what we term thoughts are more appropriately the *Yesod* of *Hod*, in that they are often internally sensed in terms of a representational system, such as sight or sound. One person may think in terms of pictures, another in terms of sound. For one, they may say that they "hear you loud and clear", to indicate their thought process, whilst another may "see what you mean". Thoughts, in terms of the *Hod* of *Hod*, occur even before they are clothed in such form. Meditative practices will often access a state where the mind seems to process without evidence, yet leaving one aware that issues are being dealt with, often more efficiently than the garbled, over-layered, process we usually call thinking.

Kabbalah teaches us to respect both reason and emotion, being aware of the nature of both in equal measure. In fact, given that many perceive Kabbalah as a very mental or intellectual pursuit, it may be surprising to read that Kabbalah does not give primacy to reason, but as Rabbi Zevi Elimelech of Dynow wrote in the 19th, understand that "reason itself shows us its limits".[76]

In terms of the creative process of the Tree of Life, *Hod* represents the first formations of the influx of energies from *Netzach*. Utilising the matrix of *Binah*, and the discriminatory processes of *Geburah*, the *Sephirah* of *Hod* crystallises these energies into definitions and

---

[76] Safran, A. *Wisdom of the Kabbalah*, p. 106.

shapes. The internal model of *Yesod* then recognises these definitions and presents them to the perceptions, as best it can to its own limits. It is thus important that the Initiate refines both his definitions and his internal model, to reflect the higher *Sephiroth* more accordingly, and become a lightning rod or watercourse for the divine energies to run through without obstruction.

In terms of the Golden Dawn system of Initiation, much of the work done at the Practicus level of *Hod* is Hermetic experimentation in order to define the limits of one's own nature, the possibilities of the environment, and the ranges of actions potential between the two, but the work of the Philosophus in *Netzach* is then to examine this work and remove contradictions thus discovered in the model of *Yesod*.

When *Yesod* is thus refined, the strait and narrow way to *Tiphareth* is accessed, and the whole Work is then returned to again, but now in order to allow the upper *Sephiroth* their full expression.

Hod is spelt in Hebrew HVD, Heh-Vau-Daleth, and totals to 15 by Gematria. This is also the Mystic Number of *Geburah*, being the summation of 1+2+3+4+5, and points to a close relationship between the two. The letters of *Hod* are symbolised by the tarot cards of the Emperor, the Hierophant, and the Empress. One could see in this the marriage of the Emperor and Empress by the Hierophant, symbolising the experience of *Hod* on a mystical level.

The cards of the paths connecting *Hod* to its companion *Sephiroth* of the Tree are as follows in the Golden Dawn system:

Hanged Man (Geburah)

The Hanged Man represents consciousness drowned in matter as one meaning of the image of the Sacrificed God, and as the Initiate progresses up the Tree, *Hod* is where he first accesses any of the *Sephiroth* above *Tiphareth*, self-awareness.

Devil (Tiphareth)

In order to rescue that consciousness, the Adept must come to terms with the primal forces represented by the Devil, but also unchain his model from his prior perceptions, which is also indicated by this card. The Devil is beaten by looking him straight in the eye (*Ayin*, the letter attributed to the Devil card).

Tower (Netzach)

The Tower connecting *Hod* to *Netzach* shows the dramatic tension that resides between these two *Sephiroth*. The relationship of one's thoughts to ones feelings is often a disharmonious one, thus causing the destruction of the Tower. However, this friction can be utilised by the Initiate in order to work on his psyche and perceptions and to build a Tower of Singular Language, not merely another Tower of Babel.

Sun (Yesod)

The Mind can reflect from *Tiphareth* experiences of a higher order, and such is often termed Gnosis by contemplatives. This illuminates the psyche, centred in *Yesod*, through the path of the Sun Atu. It is interesting to note that this functional Triad utilises the Devil Atu as Lucifer, the Light-Bringer.

Last Judgement (Malkuth)

The Last Judgement Atu shows the resultant flow of energies down the Pillar of which *Hod* is the base. From Understanding and Discrimination, and the processes of the Intellect, reflecting the arc of Will, comes the decision to act, the judgement from which flows the Will into the World of Action, *Malkuth*. If the Lower *Sephiroth* are harmonised, this will also flow from the emotions (*Netzach*) and unconscious desires (*Yesod*), otherwise conflicts will be set up on the path of the Blasted Tower, and the action will ultimately result in nothing. Imbalance in this Triad is often reflected on the other side of the Tree in the path governed by the Moon, denoting a negative side to the card's symbolism, where the cyclic repetitions of an action are caused by indecision on the other side of the Tree.

Adin Steinsaltz calls one attribute of *Hod* "perseverance".[77] This is echoed by Regardie's injunction in the introduction to the collected works of the Golden Dawn, where he states that persistence and determination alone are omnipotent. Crowley's phrase saying that work alone has ultimate value can also be allocated to the *Sephirah* of *Hod*. It is here that the Work is performed, to counter the inertia that the Ego (symbolised in this instance by the Moon on the other side of the Tree) can summon.

The Mercurial qualities of the *Sephirah* are as numerous as the symbols denoting that elusive element. It is as Sturzaker states, "the sphere of intrigue", and also of the diplomat, the thief, the scientist and the magician.[78] The sciences are rooted here, as they seek knowledge by division and mechanisms, and by strict definitions of qualities, events, and behaviours. These are all the processes of *Hod*. It might be noted here that the classical sciences are now being transcended by the new sciences of Quantum Physics, Turbulence Physics, and the mathematics of Dynamic Systems, all of which reflect more the qualities of *Netzach*, where the divisions of *Hod* have not yet taken place, and more wholeness exists. This progression has also occurred in medicine with the advent of holistic therapies. The Tree suggests that the future will bring even more integration of arts and sciences as we approach the *Tiphareth* of this development.

EXERCISES

1. Observe the composition of a thought by asking oneself, or another, "What do I think of ...?" How much of the thought complex is; an item of fact, an emotional charge, a value judgement, an image, a reference to another thought, a memory, and so on? How would this be modelled by Kabbalah?

2. Take any number of names of objects, and note what thought associations you have with them. Make a connection between this

---

[77] Steinsaltz, A. *The Thirteen Petalled Rose*, p. 61.
[78] Sturzaker, J. *Kabbalistic Aphorisms*, p. 31

and the biblical story of Adam naming the Animals. Read *The Greater Trumps* by Charles Williams in this context.

3. Note a few examples of the power of a word in your own life. Expand this exercise to historical or present examples in the social sphere around you, and the political sphere. Note examples of the Magic of language to affect our awareness.

Yesod: The Hall of Mirrors

Yesod means "Foundation", and also "base, ground, principle or compilation". It is the base of the third and final triad of the Tree, and stands between *Tiphareth* and *Malkuth* on the Middle Pillar. It is also connected directly to *Hod* and *Netzach*.

The letters of *Yesod*, *Yod-Samekh-Vau-Daleth*, total to 80 by Gematria, which is the value of *Peh*, meaning 'mouth'. The *Sephirah* is one of communication from above to below, and we should seek to align our words to our highest principles as part of our work equilibrating this *Sephirah*.

Eighty is also the value of KS, meaning 'throne', and MVLD, 'birth, or new moon'. The *Sephirah* is the lower throne of all that precedes it, and the throne of our psyche and ego-process, which (like the Moon) reflects the light of awareness, the Sun, corresponding to *Tiphareth*.

As the Moon is the planet attributed to *Yesod*, it is interesting to note that *Peh* spelt in full is *Peh-Aleph*, which totals 81, and is as Crowley states "a mystic number of the moon", as it totals 8+1=9, the number of *Yesod*, and equates with KSA, meaning again, 'throne' and also 'time of the full moon'. This number, 81, is also the value of ANKI, meaning 'ego', which again is attributed to *Yesod*. Thus both 80 and 81 represent these similar aspects of *Yesod*.

The attribution of throne and ego to *Yesod* are of note in light of the description by the Golden Dawn of the tasks undertaken by an *Adeptus Minor* (attributed to *Tiphareth*), where the ego is seen as enthroned in human consciousness as an usurpation, and the task is to return the correct functioning to each of the aspects of the psyche from this fallen state, where "the light shineth in the darkness, but the darkness comprehendeth it not."

The connection of *Peh*, the 'mouth', to *Yesod* is interesting in that upon Jacob's Ladder, *Yesod* of one Tree overlaps the *Da'ath* of the next, and thus the *Yesod* of *Yetzirah*, the ego, overlaps the *Da'ath* of *Assiah*, the throat from which we communicate our persona through our words. Hence our mouth is the gate to our ego in the way that our eyes are said to be the gates to our soul.

The letters of *Yesod* (YSVD) relate to the tarot cards of the Hermit, Temperance, the Lovers and the Empress. These cards express some of the key features of this *Sephirah*:

Hermit: The individual nature of the personal ego, but the light of the True Self is but a spark in the Lamp. This state of wandering in the darkness is enacted in the Golden Dawn Initiation Rite of Neophyte, where the candidate is blindfolded and led about the Temple by the "symbolic light of occult science", which in turn refers to their own enlightened awareness (*Tiphareth*).

Temperance: The tarot key attributed to the path leading from *Yesod* to *Tiphareth* in the initiatory progression up the Tree. As Sallie Nichols describes, "The action of the Angel Temperance as she works with the waters of the hero's psyche is like that of the sun, Nature's alchemist, on our earth's waters...". [79] The Sun is here the awakened awareness of *Tiphareth*.

Lovers: The Lovers may relate to the carnal aspects of *Yesod* as being symbolic of the generative powers of this *Sephirah*, but on a higher level relate to the choice of progression from the ego-dominated world into the self-aware one. The angel of Temperance again presides over this choice, and in the older decks is shown by a man choosing between two women (or choosing whether to be associated with one woman or not, with the advice of another, depending on one's interpretation of the glyph), and in the Waite-Smith deck by the biblical Garden of Eden, where this choice is made as the original sin of the Christian mythology.

---

[79] Nichols, S. *Jung and Tarot*, p. 258.

Empress: The Empress embodies Nature, and thus relates to the generative aspect of *Yesod* as the foundation or ground of all growth. It is important that *Yesod* is maintained as a firm foundation, otherwise the state of the Blasted Tower is brought about continually, and ones interactions with the world of *Assiah* (*Malkuth*) become confused and ultimately destructive. Thus the ego is transcended, but not destroyed in the Initiate's progression. The ego is the process governing our interaction with the environment, and thus need only be calibrated, not wiped out. This is in one sense why no behaviour is ultimately necessary to the Initiate, and why the system can be expressed differently by different individuals, cultures, and times. *Yesod*, the ego, is the filter by which the system is expressed, and not the root of it.

Yesod is also the *Sephirah* of our beliefs, both conditioned or adopted, which form the foundations of our psyche and influence our behaviour. As the lower extreme of the Tree is approached, the *Sephiroth* tend to merge, as they do at the higher extreme, and so *Yesod* tends to blend into the functions of *Netzach* and *Hod*. For example, "you are what you think", or "you are what you feel" both relate to the *Yesod* of *Hod* and *Netzach*.

Beliefs are relative, and can be utilised as garments and masks as deemed necessary. As Crowley says in *Liber Al vel Legis*, "A king may choose his garments as he will, a beggar has no choice." Other types of representational systems are also attributed to *Yesod*. These are Cosmologies, Maps, Models and Paradigms.

Cosmologies: A cosmology is an integrated set of concepts about the Universe, and has two aspects. A physical cosmology is a conceptual map of the formation and structure of the universe, whereas a metaphysical cosmology further relates to our place and role within the environment.

Maps: Maps are usually historical, in that they are descriptions of a place or places already experienced, and are drawn to guide others. Note that a map does not per se contain any indications of where one ought to go, or indeed the best way to get there. A map only serves to indicate possible routes. Usually the scale of the map needs attention, as an atlas and a street-map both serve different needs.

Models: Usually, a model is a three-dimensional or conceptual map, but as well as being descriptive, it is informative. A model tends to show not only what is, but how it works. By making a model of a system (Systems Analysis), one can then vary components of the process and view likely outcomes based on the model. This enables businesses, for example, to predict the likely outcome of stocks remaining at the end of a year if they bought new machinery, or increased staffing, and so forth. In the psyche, we all carry models of other people, *introjected* in our minds. Thus, we can work out the likely outcome of saying something to someone, or the reactions someone might have to a certain event. Our models of other people are often woefully inadequate, and indeed, our models of ourselves are often at variance to our actual behaviour. All this is the function (or dysfunction) of *Yesod*.

Paradigms: A paradigm is the set of assumptions underlying a cosmology. For example, the Newtonian Physics were based in a paradigm where the observer and environment were absolutely separate, and scientific truth could be arrived at by increasing reductionism. The new Physics are being generated from a new paradigm, where it is recognised that the actual act of observation can influence that which is observed. The event responds to our instruments of measurement, and thus, the actual event in itself remains unknown, and will always do so. This is, if you like, scientific proof of the Kabbalistic model, where *Tiphareth* can never directly be aware of *Malkuth*, except through *Yesod*, our "measuring". The new sciences are also based in a more holistic model, where systems theory replaces reductionism, and events are seen in the light of their relationships to the rest of the system, and not as isolated functions.

The deities corresponding to *Yesod* relate to varying characteristics of the *Sephirah* as follows:

Air: The Middle Pillar having attributed to it the element of Air, *Yesod* is the realm of sky-gods such as the Greek Zeus.

Foundation: By its meaning and placement on the Tree, *Yesod* as Foundation has such Gods as Ganesha and Shu, like Atlas, supporting the world, or heavens. The Grade-sign of the Golden Dawn for this *Sephirah* is that of Shu supporting the firmament.

Moon: As its primary symbol is that of the Moon, *Yesod* has attributed to it such Lunar deities as Diana. Also, in its generative aspect (merging to *Netzach*), Diana-Artemis of Epheseus, the Many-Breasted.

Threshold: As the connective element between the *Nephesch* (animal instinct) and *Ruach* (reasoning principle), such Gods as Hermanubis (Hermes the Guide and Anubis the Guardian) and Ganesha (as breaker-down of obstacles, the Juggernaut) can be placed here, as well as the Guardian of the Threshold. This latter entity is encountered as the first "fear" on the new Initiate's path, and usually manifests as the Shadow in terms of Jungian Psychotherapy. The appearance of the Guardian is the sure sign that the work of the Zelator is building up towards initiation, and not merely being used as a form of escapism.

In terms of the Creative Process down the Tree, both *Yesod* as meaning 'compilation', and the process of arrangement (from Crowley in *777*), can be placed here. The synthesis embodied in the Universe Atu leading from *Yesod* to *Malkuth* has not taken place, merely the elements of that synthesis collected. Thus is *Yesod* a "treasure-house of images", in that the actual information of these images will depend on one's own arrangement of them through the Universe Atu, or one's own Cosmology.

EXERCISES

1. Make a list of some of the beliefs that you hold, from the mundane to the exotic. You might like to list them in sets of themes, such as "Beliefs about life", "Beliefs about myself", "Beliefs

about money", and so forth. The beliefs can range from the obvious, "I believe that things fall down when I drop them", to the obtuse; "I believe that cats go to heaven but dogs don't".

2. Can you arrange your beliefs together in a tree diagram, such as shown below, where each belief depends on the beliefs above it as this example:

> 1. I believe that the Universe is a place where we should live well if we can.
>
> 2. I believe that I and my family have the right to live well.
>
> 3. I believe that I should look after the material needs of my family and myself.
>
> 4. I believe that I should stay healthy.
>
> 5. I believe that I should go to work and earn money.

Thus, one set of beliefs hangs from another more central belief.

3. Read the whole of *Prometheus Rising* by Robert Anton Wilson and try some of the exercises in that book, particularly that of finding pennies, for a full examination of the nature of our inner artist.

Malkuth: The Kingdom of the Shells

> The tenth path is called the Resplendent Intelligence because it is exalted above every head and sits upon the throne of *Binah*. It illuminates the splendours of all the lights, and causes an influence to emanate from the Prince of Countenances, the Angel of *Kether*.

> *Sepher Yetzirah*

Malkuth, in Hebrew MLKVTh (Mem, Lamed, Kaph, Vau, Tau), translates as 'Kingdom' and is the name of the tenth *Sephiroth* of the Tree of Life. An examination of the letters that compose this word may shed light upon the nature of the kingdom itself. This can be done in three ways; numerically; by analysis of the translation of the letters; and by an examination of the tarot cards to which those letters are attributed in the Golden Dawn system.

The numerical analysis provides us with MLKVTh = 40 + 30 + 20 + 6 + 400 = 496.

One common method of numerology totals the integers repeatedly until a single digit is acquired. In the case of *Malkuth*, this results in 4 + 3 + 2 + 6 + 4 = 19 = 1 + 9 = 10, the number of *Malkuth* on the Tree. Also, this further reduces to 1 + 0 = 1, the number of *Kether*, thus reminding us that *Malkuth* is in *Kether*, and *Kether* is in *Malkuth*, but after a different manner. This is the Kabbalistic equivalent to the Hermetic principle of "As above, so below". So *Malkuth* is both itself and *Kether*, by numerology, signifying the ground of reality is one and the same as the divine world.

Another method of numerology we can apply in *gematria* is to take the first and last letters of a word and use their summation. The first and last letters of *Malkuth* are *Mem* (40) and *Tau* (400), both of which are extensions of 4, the value of *Daleth*. As Aleister Crowley points out in his *Essay Upon Number*, 4 relates to "the solid existing in Time, matter as we know it."[80] So we read this as indicating that

Malkuth is the development of the letter *Daleth*; that reality is constructed of time and space, and the four elements. As Plato states in *Timaeus*, time is the moving likeness of eternity.

When we apply this to our tarot, we can also see that the card numbered four in the Major Arcana is the Empress, the illustration of nature herself. In this she corresponds to *Malkuth*, and as the *Shekinah*, the presence of the divine in the world, seen as feminine.

In further and more complex *gematria* we can also analyse the full value of 496 as 4 x 124; that is to say, the number of manifestation (4) acting upon the number of Eden (A'aDN=124), the archetypal garden of creation. In *Malkuth* then, the perfect Garden of Eden manifests itself, although we see it in *Yesod*, through a glass, darkly. As we build up and explore these resonances between numbers, symbols and our experience of the world, and through myths and illustrations, we are creating in ourselves a structured and ordered system. This system comprehends experience in an increasingly unified way, promoting wider and accelerated learning, and above all driving us to an inner sense of unity as these concepts continue to collapse towards a singular realisation.

It may be that suddenly, one morning, we awake, and find ourselves after all, in that perfect garden – a garden that was there all the time.

Those first and last letters of *Malkuth* also spell MTh 'To die, corpse, man' and in reverse, ThM, 'Complete, perfect, whole'. This suggests the nature of the *Sephirah* of *Malkuth* microcosmically as the world of man and death, and macrocosmically as the completion of the universal process as a whole system. As we revolve around these letter-plays, we often find increasingly profound processes which provoke our awareness to universal patterns.

As extensions of the number 4 (*Daleth*), Mem and *Tau* reveal another aspect of *Malkuth* which is important to the practical

---

[80] Crowley, A. *777 and other Qabalistic Writings*, p. 27.

Kabbalist. That is, *Daleth* signifies 'a gate, portal, means of passing through', and *Malkuth* has amongst its titles 'The Gate, the Gate of Tears and the Gate of Death'. This suggests, as does the recurrent reduction of *Malkuth* down to *Kether*, that the perceived world about us is the presentation of *Kether* to us, and the means by which *Kether* is communicated to our senses in much the same way a poem or piece of music is the portal to a wealth of abstract meanings and experience.

As we follow our exploration of the number 400 (*Tau*) which is also the letter on the lowest path of the Tree, connecting *Yesod* to *Malkuth* itself, we see that it is taken to show the powers of YHVH on the material plane. So the powers of 4, 40 and 400 are the four elements represented at varying levels of functionality from their most divine source to their lowest manifestation. In practical magical work, we would use these numbers as structure in any working for manifestation, perhaps by having an invocation which was composed of three parts, with four hundred words recited at the opening of the ritual, then a later prayer of forty words and then just four words at the climax of the ceremony.

In the Golden Dawn system, Malkuth is the only *Sephirah* to be split into a four-colour scheme, to reflect the four elements operating separately in Malkuth. As we pass through these elemental grades in our spiritual journey, the Golden Dawn said these first initiations "in one sense, quit not Malkuth". We remain in manifestation throughout the spiritual journey.

In his examination of the numerological codes of the Kabbalah, Carlos Suarès brings together these ideas of 4, 40 and 400 and we can apply them to *Malkuth*:

> The physical resistance of structures (4) finds its purveyor in the maternal waters (40) where all life originates. Tau (400) is the exaltation of the entire cosmic existence in its utmost capacity to resist life-death. The root DM is 'blood' in Hebrew, and the root MTh is 'death'. Thus the two together express the complete cycle of existence.[81]

We can next explore the meaning of the letters composing the title, and move on from a purely numerological analysis. The extensions of the letters composing *Malkuth* and their meanings are as follows:

Mem: The element of water

Lamed: The process of learning, defining

Kaph: The concept of hollowness (as in weighing in the hand)

Vau: The objects of fastening, pin, hook

Tau: The making of a mark, a cross

From these meanings we might deduce that the Kingdom begins symbolically and actually in the primal waters (and the Kingdom of the conscious Self is but an island in the sea of the unconscious) and completes as the cross of the four elements, traditionally Earth, Air, Fire, Water, in the manifest world about us.

There is a more beautiful example of mystical symbolism that appears to have been written into the world when we take a more literal and simple analysis of the five Hebrew letters *Mem + Lamed + Kaph + Vau + Tau* that comprise the word *Malkuth*. These are literally Water + Goad + Palm of Hand + Nail + Cross. This may remind us of a particular mythic story and yet how can that be? The very letters used to denote our world contain within themselves the most fundamental story of a religious belief about this world.

The four elements and their crowning by Spirit as the fifth (to make the Pentagram, which redeems YHVH to YHShVH) are echoed in modern mathematical ideas such as the model used by Rudy Rucker (the four concepts of Number, Space, Logic, Infinity, and the fifth, Information), and in Quantum Physics there is a similar four-fold system (Electro-Magnetism, Weak Force, Strong Force, and

---

[81] Suarès, C. *The Qabala Trilogy*, p. 58.

Gravity). The pattern of four arising to five appears fundamental in our experience of the universe.

We can now see how *Malkuth* might be illustrated by our tarot. The cards to which the letters of *Malkuth* are assigned in the Golden Dawn system are:

Mem: The Hanged Man

Lamed: Justice

Kaph: The Wheel of Fortune

Vau: The Hierophant

Tau: The Universe

Malkuth, the kingdom, begins quite appropriately, with the Hanged Man, the card symbolic of initiation and sacrifice. It is even more illustrative in its Golden Dawn variant as the drowned giant, the slumbering aspect of the divine under the waters of creation. It was this version too that Waite used in his Waite-Trinick Tarot. The card also reminds us that awareness is drowned in that flood, and as is spoken in the Neophyte ritual of the Golden Dawn, "the light shineth in the darkness, but the darkness comprehendeth it not."

The next card of the sequence is that of Justice, or as Crowley re-titled it, Adjustment. The placement of this card on the Tree connects it between *Geburah* (discernment) and *Tiphareth* (awareness) on the path of *Lamed* (discipline). Following on from the initial *Mem* stage, we may see this step as the organisation and adjustment inherent in the universal processes.

Moving on from the process of continual adjustment, we add the spin of the Wheel of Fortune, that is to say, the action of time and the circular or spiral force that can be seen in everything from the DNA helix, the conch shell, a whirlpool, a body in orbit, or an entire galaxy. The hub of the wheel, the spokes and the rim also signify synchronicity, a term coined by Carl Jung to denote an accausal connecting principle in play within all things. It is in more simple terms, a revolution; of thought, action, or of any state.

These first few cards illustrate through correspondence an evolutionary process from the initiation of the beginning, through its organisation and regulation, into connection and movement. This is a fundamental and universal pattern played out in every layer of creation from the microscopic to the cosmological.

The next card in the sequence is that of the Hierophant, he who reveals the sacred things, and subtitled by the Golden Dawn as "the expounder of the Mysteries". The Hierophant in this context represents the interface between the individual and the world as it is shown in the previous cards. It might be summarised as; Nature, all things hid reveals. The card illustrates the revelation of reality when we closely examine nature and ourselves.

If we take this card as symbolic of the individual's relationship with Nature in its widest sense, then that revelation is revealed to follow three principles to which the Hierophant must attain:

> Awareness (Hanged Man)
>
> Balance (Justice)
>
> Synchronicity (Wheel)

These three principles place the Hierophant in the middle pillar of the Tree of Life as representing *Tiphareth*, the centre in which awareness and balance are attained and synchronicity becomes a constant and ever-present quality of the initiated life. It is also a constant revolution (Wheel) and adjustment (Justice) to change in awareness (Hanged Man) as the initiatory life.

In the final letter of the word *Malkuth*, we arrive at *Tau* which corresponds quite neatly to the World card, sometimes called the Universe. This self-referential termination of the sequence demonstrates the nature of the card itself and the whole synthesis of the previous cards in manifestation. The final letter is the final summation of the universe and all things within it. The Kingdom is complete within itself and this is the truth of the matter.

Umberto Eco writes of this as he concludes *Foucault's Pendulum*:

> Where have I read that at the end, when life, surface upon surface, has become completely encrusted with experience, you know everything, the secret, the power, and the glory, why you were born, why you are dying, and how it could have been different? You are wise. But the greatest wisdom, at that moment, is knowing that your wisdom is too late. You understand everything when there is no longer anything to understand.

> Now I know what the Law of the Kingdom is, of poor, desperate, tattered Malkhut, where Wisdom has gone into exile, groping to recover its former lucidity. The truth of Malkhut, the only truth that shines in the night of the Sefirot, is that Wisdom is revealed naked in Malkhut, and its mystery lies not in existence but in the leaving of existence. Afterward, the Others begin again.

> And with the others, the Diabolicals, seeking abysses where the secret of their madness lies hidden.[82]

In summary then, we can create a magical formula of our experience of the world through the letters that comprise its title, *Malkuth*. These can be then expressed as a process of Initiation; Adjustment; Revolution; Revelation and Synthesis. All things follow this one pattern and it is useful to recognise it underneath any question brought to us as tarot readers, as we ask at which stage of this process is the client, and at which stage is the situation?

Having looked at the *Sephiroth* in turn from *Kether* to *Malkuth*, we now turn our attention to several other concepts used within Kabbalah, beginning with the *Klippoth*, the shells of the creative process.

---

[82] Eco, U. *Foucault's Pendulum*, p. 640.

EXERCISES

1. Take any science, such as Maths, Economics, Physics, or some other methodology of studying the world around us, such as Sociology or Psychology, and examine its structure in terms of the *Sephiroth* on the Tree of Life.

2. There are many further aspects of Kabbalah that go beyond the scope of this present book. You may like to explore the following list of specific concepts to deepen your appreciation of Kabbalah beyond the Tree of Life.

- *Tzimtzum*, the contraction of *Ain Soph Aur* to create *Kether*, the first point.
- *Shevirat HaKelim,* the shattering of the vessels.
- *Teshuvah* refers to a returning - a rectification of action to Divine Will.
- *Tikkun*, the state of perfection, and the spiritual process of reaching that state.
- *Kavanah,* intention, any willed act, and a form of meditation in action.

The Klippoth: The Shells & Husks

... or perhaps the seashells — the qelippot, the beginnings of ruin — were slyly waiting in ambush somewhere.

"Slippery folk, those qelippot," Belbo said. "Agents of the diabolical Dr. Fu Manchu. And then what happened?"

And then, Diotallevi patiently explained, in the light of Severe Judgement, or Gevurah — also known as Pachad, or Terror — the Sefirah in which, according to Isaac the Blind, Evil first shows itself, the seashells acquired a real existence.

"Then the seashells are in our midst," Belbo said.

"Just look around you," Diotallevi said.

Umberto Eco, *Foucault's Pendulum*, pp. 219-20.

The word *Klippoth* [variously transliterated such as Qlippoth, Kellipot, etc.] is the plural of the Hebrew word spelt Qoph-Lamed-Peh-Heh, meaning shell, husk, skin, peel or rind. This indicates at once that the Klippoth are the shells or leftovers of a process, in the same way that an eggshell is related to an egg, or the peel related to an apple. In the cosmology of Kabbalah, these shells or envelopes were said to hold their original abode beneath the world of Assiah into which Adam descended at the Fall. Thus they are not only at the base of the Tree, but somehow below it, like a dark shadow or the husks on a threshing room floor.

Much of the development of this idea was made by Issac de Loria (1534-1572) who in his commentary on the *Book of Concealment* added his own viewpoint to the original Zoharic teachings on the Klippoth.

Commenting on the formation of the nations of the gentiles, Loria said that the *recrements*, the evil and rejected parts of the Edomite Kings (who existed in the void before the world was formed) are the cortices or shells which compose the adverse Adam Belial, or the "shadow" side of humanity. When Adam and Eve partook of the forbidden fruit, their Fall confounded the Good and the Evil of the cortices, and after this Fall the nations of the world were produced from the shells. In this we can see some reflection of the politics of the age, and the history of the Jewish people, but also a commentary on the nature of the Pysche, which in its "fall" or attachment to the apparent world, forms many identities from the beliefs that in truth are the shells which separate us from recognition of our inherent "core".

The unbalanced forces of the Universe, the world in its void state, are considered under the symbolism of the Kings who reigned in Edom before a King was raised up to rule over the children of Israel, that is to say, before the emanation of the *Microprosopus*, or Lesser Countenance. This single King or state is that which reigns after the synthesis of the multiple fragmentary states of identity that flicker in and out in the constant picture-show of our awareness, each of which in its turn demands temporary rulership.

The Edomite Kings were seen by Loria as Sons of the Mother, the Pillar on the left hand, perfect Severity, but had no foundation in the Holy Ancient One. They are the "empty lights" dispelled by the Source of Lights which is concealed within the Mother.

Halevi states that the first origin of the concept of the *Klippoth* lies in the Kabbalistic model of the Universe itself being composed of a series of shells. The first kernel is the light of *Ain Soph*, with the first shell being *Kether*, enclosing *Ain Soph*. Then *Kether* becomes the kernel of the Shell which is *Chockmah*, and so on. Beyond the *Malkuth* of *Assiah* come the thickest of the shells, with hardly any of the light of *Ain Soph* in them.

In terms of the Practical Kabbalah, the 'husks' are depicted as the singular enemy of the Kabbalist. As Rabbi Chaim Vital (1543-1620) states, when talking about the decline in Kabbalistic practice:

> ... they [the practitioners] no longer make use of these techniques to ascend to the orchard ... people only make use of the techniques involving the Universe of Assiah. Since this is the lowest of the Universes, its angels have only a little good, and are mostly evil. Besides this, it is a level where good and evil are closely entwined, and it is very difficult to separate them. This does not bring any enlightenment, since it is impossible to perceive good alone, and one's perceptions are therefore a combination of good and evil, truth and falsehood. Even if one does gain some perception, it is truth intermingled with falsehood ... since one cannot purify himself, the uncleanness of the husks attaches itself to the individual who attempts to gain enlightenment by the practical Kabbalah.[83]

Therefore, "he who watches his soul should keep far from these things". Unfortunately, the rise of practical occultism in recent times has repeated the aforementioned error, and has taken the concept of the *Klippoth* into the realms of personified beings. Once this has been done, it is easy to see how practitioners may attempt to work with the *Klippoth*, and yet in reality be themselves worked by them.

In the glossary of his Magnum Opus, *Magick in Theory and Practice*, Aleister Crowley defines *Klippoth* as "shells or demons, the excrement of ideas", and it is this definition that has permeated the

---

[83] Kaplan, A. *Meditation and Kabbalah*, p. 40.

workings of such groups as the Typhonian Order with respect to the *Klippoth*. Indeed, in recent publications by the late Head of that Order, Kenneth Grant (1924 – 2011), the *Klippoth* are associated with the "shades of the dead whose names appear in the books of Dyzan, or Thoth, of the Necronomicon..." and similar grimoires.[84] The organisation of these entities into hierarchies is post-Zoharic, and found popularity with the publication of Francis Barrett's *The Magus* in 1801, which was composed of many tables indicating the structure of the Universe.

Z'ev ben Shimon Halevi points out that any event or being can become *Klippothic* if its central axis or reason for being is removed, causing imbalance in the system. Thus tradition is *klippothic* if it is merely blind observance of a form of ritual or belief which no longer unites with its original source. As such, tradition is indeed a shell or screen which separates us from reality, the wrapping and not the present itself. In a personal sense, when someone becomes obsessed as a result of a personality disorder, then the *Klippoth* are at work, as the individual then has no central point to come back to in order to regain themselves.

Another view of the *Klippoth* can be found in Roald Dahl's fantasy, *Charlie and the Glass Elevator*, where Willy Wonka's glass elevator, which, like the Chariot of the mystics, can travel through many worlds, passes through a shadowy place wherein exist hosts of grey wraithlike entities formed from all the uncompleted thoughts and hopes of mankind. Each time an individual thinks, "If only ...", they create a *Klippothic* world which begins to separate them from the actual world existing around them. If the Many Worlds interpretation of Quantum Physics is correct, then every time we make a decision, an infinite number of *Klippothic* worlds are created where that decision was not taken, and we must be careful to live in the world we have chosen.

---

[84] Grant, K. *Outside the Circles of Time*, p. 287. Grant also comments that "we are only now beginning to understand that these names [of the Qliphoth] contain formulae of immense magical and scientific potency".

Some authors see the *Klippoth* as simple reversals or negative polarities to each of the *Sephiroth*. Thus, Gray gives the *Klippothic* form of *Malkuth* as materialism, and that of *Geburah* as cruelty, and so on. The four elements themselves have *Klippoth*:

Fire: Arrogance

Air: Superfluous talk

Water: Cupidity

Earth: Melancholy

The Golden Dawn society had this to say in their Theoricus ritual:

> Be thou therefore as prompt and active as the Sylphs, but avoid frivolity and caprice. Be energetic and strong like the Salamanders, but avoid irritability and ferocity. Be flexible and attentive to images like the Undines, but avoid idleness and changeability. Be laborious and patient like the Gnomes but avoid grossness and avarice.[85]

As well as a reversal of the personal aspect of the *Sephirah*, the *Klippoth* can represent a reversal of the essential nature of each of the *Sephiroth*. Thus, the *Klippothic* form of *Kether* is the "dual contending forces", which is the exact opposite to the idea of unity in *Kether*. The *Golochab*, attributed to *Geburah*, are Giants, like volcanoes, symbolising tyranny or aimless destruction, rather than the precise discernment and functional cutting away which *Geburah* should bring to any process. *Klippoth* are thus a perversion of the original energy of a thing, a waste, imbalance, or something taken to an extreme beyond its natural purpose.

During Kabbalistic work, as the Baal Shem Tov (1698 - 1760) stated, "when an extraneous thought comes to you, this is a sign that you are being cast out. But if you are wise, you can use that thought itself to bind yourself to God all the more".[86] In the words of Maggid

---

[85] Regardie, I. *The Golden Dawn*, p. 160.

Devarav Leyaakov, "these thoughts do not come by chance, but in order that you elevate them to their root".[87] This is an important part of Kabbalah in that nothing is seen as intrinsically evil, all being part of the one Tree.

The only evil is separation, and even this can be redeemed through the process of unification.

Names of the *Klippoth* by *Sephiroth*.

1. Kether	Dual Contending Forces (Twins of God)	False Gods	Satan/Moloch	*The Finishers*
2. Chockmah	Hinderers	Lying Spirits	Beelzebub	*The Life-Cutter of God*
3. Binah	Concealers (Hiding)	Vessels of Iniquity	Luciferge	*One who Hides*
4. Chesed	Breakers in Pieces (Smiters)	Revengers of Wickedness	Astaroth	*Those that are Crooked*
5. Geburah	Burners (Flaming Ones)	Jugglers	Asmodeus	*The Barber*
6. Tiphareth	Disputers (The	Airy Powers	Belphegor	*The Flayer*

[86] Kaplan, A. *Meditation and Kabbalah*, p. 286.
[87] *Ibid*, p. 290.

	Litigation)			
7. Netzach	Dispersing Ravens	Furies, or Seminaries of Evil	Baal	*Those Kindling the Funeral Pyre*
8. Hod	Deceivers (The False Accuser)	Sifters, or Triers	Addramalech	*The Venom of God*
9. Yesod	Obscene Ones (The Obscene Ass)	Tempters, or Ensnarers	Lillith	*He who Bears a Burden*
10. Malkuth	The Evil Woman (The Woman of the Night)	Wicked Fouls bearing rule	Nahema	*The Moaners*

EXERCISES

1. Take ten events and attempt to note down the *Klippothic* aspect(s) of the event, if any. For example, a mother's overweening pride of her daughter's accomplishments, a machine which was calibrated incorrectly and snaps a pipe it was meant to bend, or the noise of a car, which does not directly contribute to its forward motion.

2. Sit in a comfortable position and try to focus on one particular image, say a circle. Each time another thought or image arises, rather than trying to ignore it, follow it back to whatever concern

generated it, acknowledge that that too is part of yourself, and then return to the original contemplation. Repeat this and observe what effect this has on the arising of extraneous thoughts.

Gematria: The Numerology of the Kabbalah

Gematria is one of the rules for interpreting the Torah, and is at root a system of numerology. It is defined by Scholem as "explaining a word or group of words according to the numerical value of the letters, or of substituting other letters of the alphabet for them in accordance with a set system".[88]

As we have seen, all Hebrew letters are equally values and words, so for example the letter Aleph, signifying "A", also means "one", as well as being a word meaning "ox". This allows the letters to be taken as symbols expressing different aspects of the Universe, either as separate entities, or when combined together in words.

One use for Gematria is in devising systems of mnemonic reminders of Kabbalistic doctrine, such as utilised by Eleazar of Worms. Thus, the numeration of the word Avavah, 'love' being equal to that of Achad, 'unity' (both being thirteen) recalls to the Kabbalist that love of God is unity with God. As the two words then total together to twenty-six, which is the value of YHVH, the *Tetragrammaton*, then this indicates further that God is composed of Unity and Love. Indeed, it is with particular reference to the names of God to which Gematria is pointed, as the names are considered divine and incomprehensible.

Although some Kabbalists decried the use of Gematria, other authors such as Abulafia dealt with Gematria so deeply that their works need decoding rather than merely reading.

It is said that the *Torah* is likewise written, and that apparent mistakes in the original Greek and Hebrew texts are not mistakes, but rather spellings and variations necessary to ensure the numbers underlying them were correct. As many Occultists have used Gematria to support their own models and approaches, it is essential that where it is recognised, it is tested.

---

[88] Scholem, G. *Kabbalah*, p. 337.

The magician Aleister Crowley utilised Gematria as a testing of spirits whilst pathworking or travelling the Aeythrs in vision. That is, he would ask his scryer to present the entity to be tested with a question or a number, and the entity would be expected to reply appropriately. Thus, if a pathworking was in the realm of *Hod*, and a young boy had appeared, he might be asked about the workings of Mercury. If he replied with a number which was later discovered to be that of the word 'swiftness', his other responses would be considered valid. The theory is basically that the false spirits will not know the Gematria appropriate to the working as they are not consistent themselves with the correspondences being worked.

There are many forms of Gematria - one list gives seventy-two forms, and Moses Corovero listed nine major systems.

The most basic method is simply taking the value of the letters of a word and adding them up, then considering all the other words that total to the same value. For this purpose, many Occultists keep and maintain a *Sepher Sephiroth* or 'Book of Numbers', which functions as a numerological dictionary. The main numbers used by Crowley are to be found in many of his works, the most important numbers being 31, 93, 418 and 666. Crowley produced his own lists based on the Golden Dawn teachings, and published these as *777*. He also produced *Liber MCCLXIV*, a dictionary based on Greek words and phrases and their numerations.

As examples, a few numbers from a personal *Sepher Sephiroth* are given below:

> 10: Value of *Yod*; DAH (To fly, soar); BDD (To be secluded); AT (Soothsayer); ADH (To steam, rise skyward); Grade Password of *Chesed*; 1+2+3+4; Number of *Malkuth*; Number of Wheel tarot card

> 11: ChG (To make a circle) (Festival, feast); GCh (To break through); ChBA (To hide oneself); Crowley's number of Magick, "energy tending to change"; Number of Justice tarot card

12: GDH (Goddess of Fortune); AVH (Desire, longing); VV (The letter *Vau*, meaning pin, hook, fastening); HVA (He himself); Number of Hanged Man tarot card

13: BHV (Emptiness, chaos); ABDH (Destruction, abyss); DVG (Fisher); VHB (Pool); AChD (One, unity); AHBH (Love); 9+3+1=111 base 3; Number of Death tarot card

Another method of Gematria is to square each value, thus AGD, meaning "to bind together", becomes $1^2+3^2+4^2=26$=YHVH, the Tetragrammaton binding the four elements. This particular method, as some of the others, result in large numbers.

Perhaps one of the safest rules to apply to Gematria work was given by Nahmanides, who said, "no-one may calculate a Gematria in order to deduce from it something that occurs to him".[89] That is, avoid the temptation to produce Gematria to shore up one's own rocky beliefs. If an equation does not mean much to you, it might be worth pursuing to develop new knowledge and widen one's system, rather than merely constraining it within existing expectations.

Gematria can produce many avenues of enquiry and exploration, and there are many books on more general numerology available on the market. I offer two examples of applying simple number systems to Kabbalah and Gematria to highlight aspects of the *Sephiroth*; the Binary system and the Numbers of the Grade System.

The Binary System
The Binary system, or base two, works by denoting all numbers in terms of ones and zeroes. In order to achieve this, rather than decimal, which works in terms of ones, tens, hundreds and so forth, base two works in columns of powers of two. These can be attributed to the *Sephiroth* in succession to reveal the following meanings:

---

[89] See
https://www.jewishvirtuallibrary.org/jsource/judaica/ejud_0002_0007_0_07165.html [Last accessed 17th June 2015].

Kether	1	Value of Aleph
Chockmah	2	Value of Beth
Binah	4	Value of Daleth; also 2+2 and 2*2
Chesed	8	AHB (To love)
Geburah	16	AIH (Hawk)
Tiphareth	32	IChID (Oneness); Number of *Sephiroth* + Paths
Netzach	64	NVGH (Venus)
Hod	128	ChLTz (To deliver, loose)
Yesod	256	
Malkuth	512	

The Grade Passwords

These words, listed in Crowley's *777*, were chosen to equal numbers which are produced by simply adding cumulatively, i.e. 1, 1+2=3, 1+2+3=6, 1+2+3+4=10 and so forth. In each case I provide a brief commentary as to how this sequence of numbers and corresponding words can add to our layered understanding of the grades of the Tree of Life. I will provide for each *Sephirah* a brief contemplative phrase as to the creative process being played out down the Tree, and the initiatory/learning process up the Tree, based on this Gematria.

Kether	1	Value of Aleph
Creative:		From unity all things proceed.
Initiatory:		To unity all things return.

Chockmah	3	AB (Father, source)

Creative: The source of all things is the seed.

Initiatory: We return to the source as a child becomes a parent.

Binah 6 GG (Covering of altar); HA (Existence, airhole)

Creative: All experience is shaped by what exists underneath and beyond all experience.

Initiatory: We look through our worship to that which is worshipped.

Chesed 10 BDD (To be secluded); DAH (To fly, soar)

Creative: The divine withdraws itself even as it expands.

Initiatory: We remove ourselves from ourselves as we ascend.

Geburah 15 GZH (Shearing, fleece)

Creative: Nothing is wasted.

Initiatory: We lose all that protects us when there is nothing that we fear.

Tiphareth 21 VDAI (Certainty)

Creative: In the centre, it is all true.

Initiatory: The Adept experiences that which is being experienced.

Netzach   28   HChIH (The beast)

Creative: All that lives, lives.

Initiatory: We are more than our own nature.

Hod   36   IChIDH (Oneness)

Creative: In thought, everything is resolved to one thing.

Initiatory: As we work, we come to aspire to unity.

Yesod   45   LVT (Covering, veil)

Creative: All existence is the veil of that for which light is but a
veil.

Initiatory: We dream our self and must awaken.

Malkuth   55   KLH (Bride), DVMH (Stillness, Realm of Death)

Creative: In this moving likeness of eternity, we are wedded to
the divine.

Initiatory: The mystical life will be both wedding and funeral.

EXERCISES

1. Begin a loose-leafed folder of lined paper, and write down the margin the numbers one to about nine hundred, allowing two or three lines for each number. Then, using the values given in the table, calculate out the total value of words relating to the Tree of Life. We have already given several calculations for the titles of the *Sephiroth* and so forth, and these can be noted in your own *Sepher Sephiroth*, or 'Book of Numbers'.

Purchase or loan from a library a Hebrew-English dictionary and even better a Bible in Hebrew and English. Select words of interest and add them to their appropriate values in your folder. Note if certain numbers have themes of words. Add to this dictionary as you advance your studies, and perhaps you will find numbers being presented to you in dreams, or sets of letters which then turn out to have significance in your own personal dictionary

The Twenty-Two Paths

> Each *Sephirah* (which is the singular form of the word of which *Sephiroth* is the plural) is a phase of evolution, and in the language of the Rabbis they are called the Ten Holy Emanations. The paths between them are phases of subjective consciousness, the Paths or grades (Latin, *gradus*, step) by which the soul unfolds its realisation of the cosmos. The *Sephiroth* are objective and the Paths are subjective.
>
> Dion Fortune, *The Mystical Qabalah*, p. 37.

Kabbalah differentiates between the essential nature of the *Sephiroth* and the Paths, but also maintains their similarity in the divine process by referring to the whole system as thirty-two Paths. We have seen already in earlier chapters on the tarot how the paths represent the initiatory process and in this chapter we will look specifically at the nature of each path in terms of the Tree and the Sepher Yetzirah. We will look at the paths in sets as these groupings allow us to see some of the intricate patterns between the paths in their functioning together as a whole.

As we have seen, the immediate difference between the *Sephiroth* and the Paths is represented by the glyph of the Tree, which most often indicates the *Sephiroth* as spheres or concentric circles, and the Paths as lines or channels. We should be reminded that the word *Sephirah*, the plural of which is *Sephiroth*, does not mean 'sphere', in fact being more accurately translated as a 'numerical emanation', and it is important to recall that, like the models of molecules we see in school chemistry books, the *Sephiroth* or the Paths are not 'things', and neither do they have shapes.

Be that as it may, we must depict the process that Kabbalah describes as best we can, and as a network of open circles connected by channels we can demonstrate important properties of the universe. In an early version of what is now known in science as "string theory", small particles were modelled by an "S-Matrix theory", and were seen as intermediate states in a network of interactions, where the lines of the matrix were "reaction channels" through which energy flows.[90] In part, it attempted to show that particles are events and not things. Equally, we must see Kabbalah as a dynamic process, a verb and not a noun.

The Interaction Region inside the circles of an S-matrix is "blurred and unspecified" as one scientist put it, just as we might see it in Kabbalah. The *Sepher Yetzirah* says this of the *Sephiroth*:

> Their end is lost in infinity. The word of God moves in them; leaving and returning ceaselessly like a whirlwind, they execute the divine word in an instant...[91]

The paths, on the other hand, as Kircher puts it, are "luminous roads by which one can attain the hidden centres".[92] That is to say, the paths are the observable symptoms of the process depicted by the *Sephiroth*, but only through our knowledge of the paths can we come to appreciate the nature of the *Sephiroth*, which in themselves remain unknowable.

In a sense, we are in the position of playing a cosmic version of the children's' game of Battleships, where it is the crosses we make on the sheet of guesses every time we choose a position where the battleship is not which eventually outline the shape of the hidden vessel.

Magical Initiation is the process of removing the guesses and that which is left, as Arthur Conan Doyle has Sherlock Holmes put it,

---

[90] Zukav, G. *The Dancing Wu Li Masters: An Overview of the New Physics*, p. 266.
[91] See Westcott, W W.. *The Kabbalah* including his translation of the *Sepher Yetzirah*.
[92] Quoted in Papus, *The Qabalah*, p. 233.

"however improbable, must be the truth," or at least, certainly narrow down the area which is the truth. The algebra of initiation is that of exhaustion, division and subtraction, not of addition and multiplication.

The classic text dealing with the Paths is that found in the *Sepher Yetzirah*. However, it reads very much like a series of unintelligible Zen Koans and it may be that they are most accessible by prolonged meditation and intuition, rather than a full-frontal analytical attack.

I offer here a few notes as to their relationships in terms of the Pillars and the Triads. I have used the Golden Dawn correspondences for any tarot references. It should also be noted that the descriptions offered by the text of the *Sepher Yetzirah* seem to describe some Paths in their descending context and functions, and others in their ascending context. It may be that the *Sepher Yetzirah* was pieced together from fragmentary notes of larger, oral, commentaries.

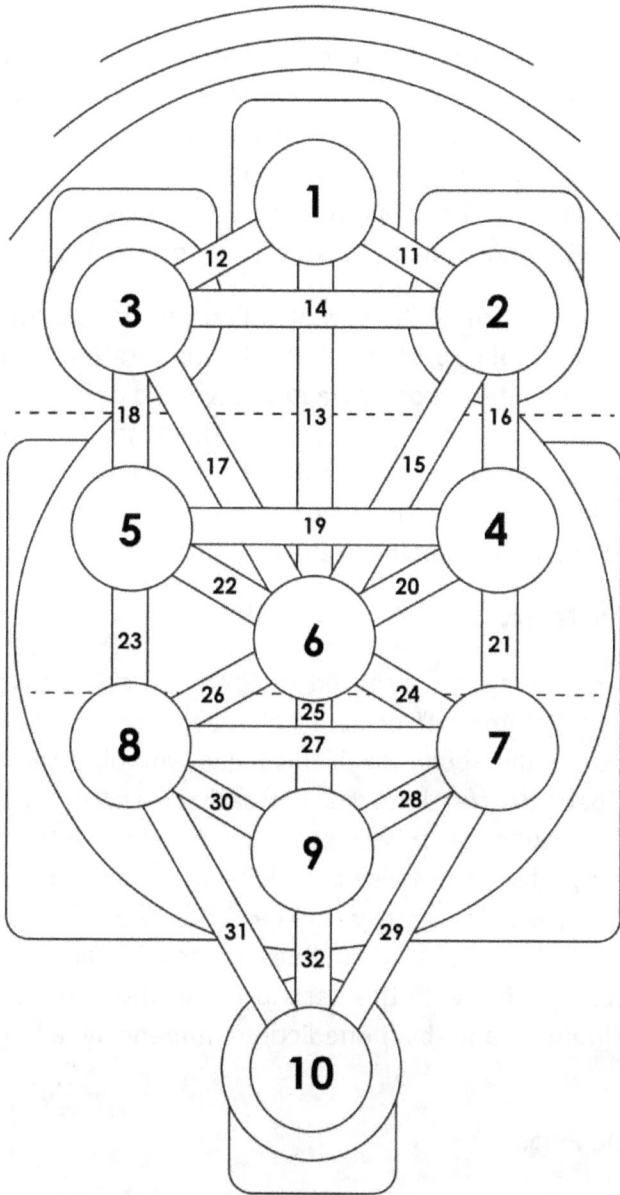

Illus. Tree of Life with Path Numbers.

The Pillar of Severity

The Pillar of Severity is composed of Paths 18 and 23, which both indicate the formative nature of the Pillar. Path 18 is described as the "House of Affluence", from which are drawn hidden meanings. This refers to *Binah*, from which the Path runs, as understanding, and *Geburah*, as discernment. With these qualities, one can discover the secret arcana or mysteries of universal processes.

The lower Path on the Pillar is that called the "Stable Intelligence", and is "the cause of consistency in all the numerations". This quality comes from the interaction of *Geburah*, with its defining nature and *Hod*, with its aspect of reverberation. The stability referred to is depicted in the tarot card attributed to this Path, which is that of the Hanged Man, which shows both judgement, in the gallows, and reverberation, in the hanging or pendulum symbol.

The Pillar of Mercy

The Pillar of Mercy is composed of Paths 16 and 21, the first of which is the "triumphal" or "eternal" Path, connecting *Chockmah* and *Chesed*. As the *Sephiroth* of this Pillar symbolise the expansive, "force" aspect of the Universe, we can see this Path shows the observable results of this expansion. *Netzach*, into which the twenty-first path leads, is also called "Victory", and of the path it is said that it "rewards those who seek". As *Chesed* means "loving kindness", and has the same qualities as the magnamanious planet-God Jupiter, this fits with the description of the Path as "receiving divine influences and by benediction influencing all things that exist".

The Middle Pillar

The Middle Pillar of Equilibrium has three paths which compose it, being Path 13, 25 and 32. In descending order, Path 13 is called "inductive of unity", path 25 the path of "trial", and path 32 the "Governing Intelligence".

The lower path, path 32, is seen in its cosmological aspect as governing the "operation of the seven planets". The tarot card attributed to this path is that of the "Universe", and its meaning is synthesis, indeed some cards show the planets as part of the symbolism of the card. In terms of the ascending process, the Path connects the world of events around us (*Malkuth*) with our own personality (*Yesod*) through the ego, and beliefs. Thus, the nature of our beliefs governs our awareness of the seven planets, as symbols of the seven *Sephiroth* below the Abyss.

The Path leading from *Yesod* to *Tiphareth*, one of whose symbols is the crucified god-man, is aptly described as the "first temptation by which god tests the devout". The last temptation is made on upon the cross of *Tiphareth* and is powerfully portrayed in the film, *The Last Temptation of Christ* (dir. Martin Scorsese, 1988).

Once *Tiphareth* has been gained, then for the first time we are brought into direct contact (although still existing in a dualistic or separated mode) with *Kether*, through Path 13. This path is described as the "substance of glory, it makes known truth to every spirit", and is depicted in this function in Aleister Crowley's Thoth deck 'High Priestess', which is attributed to this path. He does warn that "It is important for high initiation to regard Light not as the perfect manifestation of the Eternal Spirit, but rather as the veil that hides that Spirit".[93]

The Triads

(i) The Paths denoting the activity resulting as the interaction between *Kether*, *Chockmah* and *Binah* are that of Path 11, Path 12 and Path 14. Their names reflect their proximity to the "limitless light" of *Ain Soph Aur*, being entitled:

Path 11:   The Fiery Intelligence

Path 12:   The Intelligence of Light

---

[93] Crowley, A. *Book of Thoth*, p. 73.

Path 14:   The Illuminating Intelligence

Both Light and Fire, as we saw in the chapter relating to the *Ain Soph Aur*, are symbols of the Creative aspect of God, or the Universal process of generation. The early Persians venerated the Fire God as the supreme Creator God, and this probably relates to primitive associations between fire and survival. It was only in later civilisations that we moved away from fire and earth gods and began worshipping sky gods. Perhaps as our species begins to explore the vastness of space, we will develop an allegiance to water gods.

Note that Path 11 is called the Veil, and Path 12 the "Image of magnificence". Again, Kabbalah warns us that the experiences of photism we may have in mystical experience are no more reality than any other experience, and are still merely the garments of God, not the Being.

(ii) The second Triad adds the two Paths leading from the upper *Sephiroth* to *Tiphareth*, the seat of awareness. These two Paths are Path 15 and Path 17, the "Constituting" and the "Disposing" Intelligences. The first is the Path to which the Emperor card is attributed, and relates to the "Creation in warm darkness". This fits with the symbolic meaning of Aries, the generative force in Astrology, which is also attributed to the Path. On the other side of the Tree, the Lovers card symbolises the "Disposing" of occult experience through intuition, which is how the Golden Dawn saw the card, as the "impact of inspiration on intuition". That is to say, the experience in awareness of that which is above the Abyss comes not through the Intellect (*Hod*), the Emotion (*Netzach*) or the Imagination (*Yesod*), but above these faculties.

(iii) The third Triad connects *Chesed*, *Geburah* and *Tiphareth*. The Paths are Paths 19, 20 and Path 22, called as follows:

Path 19:   Secret Intelligence

Path 20:   The Will

Path 22:   The Faithful Intelligence

Path 19, the second of the Paths coming down the Tree to run horizontally across, is said to "receive fullness from the highest benediction", and to relate to "spiritual activities". We can see that as the top Path of the Triad of the three *Sephiroth* forming the transpersonal aspects of the psyche, and even the trans-conscious aspects, or pre-conscious activities, then this would be the case. In a sense, the Path also acts as a reflection in a lower order of Path 14 above it, which is the "Institutor of arcana, foundation of holiness". In more mundane terms, we can see that Path 14 refers to Nature, and Path 19 below it refers to our relationship to Nature.

Path 20 "prepares beings individually for the demonstration of the existence of Wisdom", according to the *Sepher Yetzirah*. As we have already seen, 'Wisdom' is one of the meanings of *Chockmah*, and as this Path connects *Chesed* to *Tiphareth*, we can see that *Chesed* acts as a precursor of *Chockmah*, manifesting itself to the Initiate of *Tiphareth* as loving kindness, as if to say, "there is a Wisdom governing the Universe".

The tarot card of the Path is the Hermit, and we can see that he acts as a demonstrator of Wisdom by his very being, and the Lamp he holds aloft. The fact that the Path is called "Will" is of interest in that the Hermit can be taken to represent the Way of Initiation, and in terms of the descending flow of the Tree, the expansive nature of *Chesed*. When these two aspects are merged, we gain the true essence of Will; that we are unalterably part of the process of the Universe in manifestation, and our realisation of this state is our Will, and everything else is *Klippoth*, or a shell that separates us from our actual nature.

Path 22 is that to which the Justice card is attributed, and as the *Sepher Yetzirah* states, "spiritual virtues are deposited and augmented within it". That is, the process of *Geburah* at any level or in any system is that of discernment, sorting the wheat from the chaff. This particular path is where that process is seen to be taking place, as Justice, or as Crowley re-titled the card, "Adjustment";

doing so to indicate that the card had no relation to our usual, limited, sense of justice with its connotations of ethics, politics or even common-sense, all of which are rooted in the illusionary universe about us.

(iv) The lower of the two upward-pointing triangles on the Tree is that composed of Paths 24, 26 and 27. *Tiphareth* itself is called as a Path, the "Median Intelligence", and it "multiplies the flow of emanations", acting as a *Kether* below the Veil of *Paroketh*. Whereas the three Paths of the upper triad deal with the light of Creation, these three Paths deal with the life of Creation:

Path 24:   The Imaginative Intelligence

Path 26:   The Renewing Intelligence

Path 27:   The Active Intelligence

The tarot cards which relate to these Paths are those often seen as the negative aspects of the whole deck, being Death, The Devil and The Blasted Tower. However, in the light of the Path descriptions above, we can see that they symbolise essential qualities of the Creative and Generative processes of the Universe. Path 24, that of Death, gives "Similarity to the likeness of Beings". That is, beneath and beyond the transformations taking place about us, the 'Song remains the Same', as the Led Zeppelin song puts it.

All Creatures, including ourselves, are in a sense the froth on the wave of the Universe, forever changing our manifestation, and yet always remaining part of the Wave. Our lives and deaths are like watching the patterns emerging and being re-absorbed on the surface of a wind-rippled lake. The ripples are our lives, the Water is manifestation, and the Wind is God moving across the Waters; a process which did not end at Genesis, but is part of the continual emergence of the Universe and is still happening right here and now. This awareness of the Death path is part of the result of the Vision of Beauty seen by the Adeptus Minor on attaining *Tiphareth*.

On the other side of *Tiphareth*, we have the 26th Path to which is attributed the Devil card. The Golden Dawn described this card as an image of Pan, who is the Greek God of Creativity and Generation. The Path is called the "Renewing Intelligence", and hence governs the processes of regeneration. That is to say, this Path regulates and kicks off constant cycles of activity just as the thermostat in a central heating system governs the activities of the whole system.

Path 27, the third and final Path running horizontally across the Tree is that called the "Active Intelligence". It is the "Spirit of every creature, the motion to which they are subject", and has the Blasted Tower card attributed to it. In the earlier versions of the card, it was entitled "The House of God, Struck by Lightning" and perhaps we can see a reference to the first lightning flash of creation striking the primordial soup from which life emerged. In a psychological rather than cosmological context, the Path represents the interaction of the thought process (*Hod*) and our emotions (*Netzach*), which together generate, or at least act as symptoms of the motion to which we are subject.

(v) We have just examined Path 27 with regard to the Triad of *Tiphareth*, *Netzach* and *Hod*, and now we will examine the first of two Triads coming down from those two *Sephiroth* and having Path 27 has their uppermost Path.

The first of which leads down to *Yesod*, and the second to *Malkuth*. Connecting *Hod* to *Yesod* we have Path 30, the "Collective Intelligence", and from *Netzach* to *Yesod* we have Path 28, the "Perfecting (or Natural) Intelligence". Here we begin to deal with the Stellar or Astrological aspects of the Tree, as it relates to the realm of the sky, with Air being attributed to *Yesod*. The tarot cards at the base of the Tree mirror this scheme, with Path 30 having the Sun card attributed to it, and Path 28 the Star card.

Through Path 28, the "nature of everything in the orb of the sun is completed and perfected", which refers to both basic astronomy and the fact that the "orb of the sun" symbolises the *Sephiroth* about *Tiphareth*, to which the Sun is attributed. *Netzach* represents the instincts and processes of nature, and *Yesod* represents the foundation or compilation stage of an activity or creative process. Thus this Path is where life takes on levels of meaning and is woven into a whole. The Star card shows this as the pouring forth of water, as does the Zodiacal sign of Aquarius which is also attributed to this Path and card.

On the other side of the Tree, Path 30 is where "Astrologers derive the speculations and perfection of their science according to the movement of stars". This Path is thus related to the science (*Hod*) regarding the hidden substructure (*Yesod*) of the World (*Malkuth*), and aims to comprehend the processes running through Path 28. The tarot card relating to the Path is that of the Sun which is the centre of any form of Astrology or early Astronomy.

(vi) The final Triad of the Tree is that of the Paths leading to *Malkuth*. We have already examined the central Path, and here we will look at the two Paths leading from *Hod*, Path 31, and *Netzach*, Path 29.

Through correspondence, the 31st path, between the *Sephiroth Hod* and *Malkuth*, is illustrated by the tarot card of the Last Judgment. The path is said by the *Sepher Yetzirah* to "rule the movement of the sun and moon". So the card illustrates the regulation of judgment – making decisions as to what (or whom) goes where in the universe. When we see this path and card in connection with the paths making up the lowest four positions of the Tree of Life we see a set of essential activities; the 31st path (Judgment) regulating, and the other three paths renewing, perpetuating and manifesting. This lowest area of the Tree consists of these four building-blocks of the universe, the world of activity, *Assiah*.

Finally, Path 29, to which the Moon card is attributed, "forms the bodies, and governs their growth". As the link between *Netzach*, the *Sephirah* of Nature (and its cycles) and *Malkuth*, the *Sephirah* of the World of Action, we can see that this Path would indeed be formed to regulate the corporeal aspects of manifestation. At this level the Tree is functioning as a model of biological principles and the apparent processes going on in the world around us. It is as we venture further up the paths that we gain knowledge of the unseen realms and higher orders by virtue of constantly widening our conceptual framework to accept the recognition of these levels.

We spend our life upon these twenty-two Paths, so must not expect to comprehend them individually or together in any immediate fashion. We must gradually compare our experience to their nature, learn, change our thinking, and re-engage our life in their context. We create a living experiential map of our situation and through it slowly construct and calculate a new equation; one of unity and not of separation.

EXERCISES

1. Take five Paths, and in turn look at the *Sephiroth* they connect, and work out your own images and keywords for the Path. Link these if you wish with the tarot Card, Planet, Element and so forth connected with the Path. For example, for the Path connecting *Geburah* and *Chesed*, you might have the image of a children's see-saw, a Lion-Tamer, and two Kings standing together, one a warrior and the other a ruler. Continue to build up your own *777* or Book of Correspondences with these images.

The Psyche: A Curtain of Souls

All cosmologies include some attempt to describe and model the elements that constitute the human experience and the nature, constitution and processes of the inner realm. Their complexity and lucidity varies from culture to culture, and often models are variations on a theme, or expanded versions of earlier systems. The simplest model might well be that implied in Descartes' famous dictum, *cogito ergo sum*, "I think, therefore I am."

The Self is one of the basic experiences of the human psyche, in that it is that to which we constantly refer our experience, both in the environment, for example, "I am having a cup of tea", and in our inner world, such as "I am feeling happy." It is impossible to define these two worlds as separate except in our mundane experience, in that the external world so-called is in part, if not in totality, an experience equally generated by our own internal world.

In Kabbalah, this is indicated by the separation of *Tiphareth*, Self-Awareness, to *Malkuth*, the actual world, by *Yesod*, the intermediating ego-state. Our thoughts (*Hod*) and emotions (*Netzach*) constantly alter the process of *Yesod* (Ego) in acting as our interpreter of the environment such that what we perceive is in fact our shared vision of the world, not the actual world itself. Kant expressed this in his *Prolegomena to any future Metaphysics*;

> As the senses never and in no single instance enable us to know things in themselves, but only their appearances, and as these are mere representations ... all bodies, together with the space in which they are, must be held to be nothing but mere representations in us, and exist nowhere else than merely in our thought.[94]

---

[94] Kant, E. (ed. G. Hatfield), *Prolegomena to any future Metaphysics*. Cambridge University Press: Cambridge, 2004. p. 40

The actual world is termed by Kant the *Ding-an-sich*, the "thing-in-itself". This is *Malkuth*, which in itself is also *Kether*, after another manner.

The medieval Kabbalists, such as Abraham ibn Ezra, followed on from the Neo-Platonic school of Plotinus in utilising a threefold division of the functions of the psyche. These were then mapped onto the Tree of Life in various fashions. The three primary divisions and their literal meanings are:

Nefesh	(NPSh; breath, spirit, soul, person, character in drama, tombstone)
Ru'ah	(RVCh; Wind, spirit, ghost, disposition)
Neshamah	(NShMH; breath, soul, life, living creature)

This trinity, as developed by such Kabbalists as Rabbi Moses Korduero and Rabbi Yitzchaq Loria, is usually taken to represent:

Nefesh	Animal vitality
Ru'ah	Self-awareness
Neshamah	Transcendent awareness

Eliphas Levi summarises these elements as the Passions, the Reason, and the Higher Aspirations, and puts it that "The body is the veil of the *Nephesch*, the *Nephesch* is the veil of *Ruach*, *Ruach* is the veil of the shroud of *Neschemah*".[95]

A further development of these divisions, after the original Zoharic teachings, appended the *Chiah* (ChIH: soul, life) to the system, thereby making a parallel to the four worlds:

Chiah	*Atziluth*
Neschamah	*Briah*

---

[95] Levi, E. *The Book of Splendours*, p. 157.

| Ru'ah | Yetzirah |
| Nefesh | Assiah |

A final addition to these teachings came with 13th Century occultists, when the concept of a *Yechidah* was added, referring to the ultimate spark of God within the psyche. The word comes from the root IChID, meaning 'oneness', and is a similar root to IChID, 'privacy, union with God'.

The trinity of *Yechidah*, *Chiah* and *Neschamah* were all bound up under the title of the *Neschamah*, and attributed to *Kether*, *Chockmah* and *Binah*. The *Ru'ah* was attributed to the six *Sephiroth* including and between *Chesed* to *Yesod*, and the *Nefesh* to *Malkuth*.

Crowley, in *Little Essays Towards Truth*, describes the four elements as:

Yechidah	Point, quintessential principle of soul
Chiah	Creative impulse (Will) of *Yechidah*
Ruach	Mind, spirit
Nephesch	Animal Soul

Crowley noted that the *Ruach*, centred in *Tiphareth*, reaches its culmination in *Da'ath*, the union of *Chockmah* and *Binah*, and positioned at the Abyss. Thus the ultimate transcendence of the Self is brought about by this Divine Knowledge.

Kabbalists saw their work as ultimately bringing about the descent of the *Neschamah* by the holy union of the King (*Melekh*) and Queen (*Matronita*), which refer to *Tiphareth* and *Malkuth*. As the Ramak stated in *Pardes Rimonim*:

> The *Nefesh* (Lower soul) can motivate the *Ruach* (Middle Spirit) and the *Ruach* in turn motivates the *Neshamah* (Upper soul). The *Neschamah* then ascends from one essence to the next, until it reaches its source.

The Soul in Ancient Egypt

The Kabbalah is only one of many cosmologies which attempt to describe the functions of human experience. The ancient Egyptians developed a complex system of souls inhabiting the individual, and as these may be contrasted against the Kabbalistic divisions, I will mention them here briefly.

As the Egyptian Model in earlier esotericism is often based on the works of Wallis Budge, whose writings were original at the time, but are now dated by more modern research, there are many differences of spelling and opinion as to the significance of the various elements making up the Egyptian model.

For example, the Khu is referred to by Perkins in his *Egyptian Life and the Tree of Life*, and rendered as "intelligence of divinity" attributed to *Kether*.[96] However, Khu is actually the now discredited reading of the word Akh, and is one of the spirit forms released at death, with the root meaning of "to be bright" (the Akhu are the spirits of the dead). Thus it is not applicable to divinity or *Kether* in the way Perkins sees it, as it would rather be allocated to *Yesod* in terms of the *Sephiroth* or the *Nefesh* in terms of the divisions of the Soul.

However, for further exploration and correspondence to Kabbalah I give here the divisions of the soul within the esoteric model based on the Ancient Egyptian system.

Egyptian Name	Glyph	Qualities
Khat (Kat, Xat, Kab)	Fish	Body
Sahu	Mummy & Seal	Spiritual Body
Ka (Kai)	Upraised hands	Image, Double
Ba (Baie)	Various birds	Spirit-Soul
Khaibt	Fan	Shadow, Aura

---

[96] Perkins, K. & Johnson, K. *Egyptian Life and the Tree of Life*.

Akh (Khu, Khou, Yekh)	Bennu bird	Bright Spirit
Sekhem	Owl	Vital Power
Ren	Kneeling man	Name
Hati	Lion	Whole Heart
Ab	Jar	Will
Tet (Zet)	Upright snake	Soul
Hammemit	Radiating sun	Unborn Soul

Whilst these may seem obscure and complex, they have practical use within ritual and magical acts. Florence Farr, in *Egyptian Magic*, saw these divisions acting through magical practice by influencing the Ka and the Ba in the Ab.[97]

This representation is a mirror image, she said, of the Ka reaching up to provide a resting-place for the Ba, symbolised by the Hawk. This latter is an emanation of the Hammemmit, and signified the sacrifice of the lower self to the higher self. Again, whilst the language may not be immediately accessible, Farr did offer an explanation.

In ritual, she explained the process of magic in terms of the above divisions of the soul:

(a) The symbolism of the ritual is fully recognised.

(b) The Imagination is extended to encompass this symbolism.

(c) The Will is concentrated firmly and repeatedly.

(d) The Ka (Ego) is thus put into tension, and acts on its counterpart in the heart (Ab), which is the vessel of conscious desire.

(e) This in turn reacts on the Hati (unconscious executant).

---

[97] Farr, F. *Egyptian Magic*, p. 11.

(f) The whole psyche thus in a state of theurgic excitation, the Ba (Divine Link) descended, and the whole body becomes a Khu (Shining One or Augoides).

(g) This new Being is established in the midst of the Sahu (Elemental Body), and hence by its radiation can awaken corresponding potencies in nature. The Sahu could hence be seen in modern terms as a morphogenetic field.

(h) For this purpose, the Khaibt is used as the link between the Ego and Non-ego, and the Tet (Spiritual Body) is established.

These systems are taught and experienced in magical orders such as the Order of Everlasting Day.

Other models for the psyche include Gurdjieff's scheme of the Octaves, and two other eight-fold systems, being the Psychosynthesis construct of Roberto Assagioli, M.D. and the Circuit Grid model developed by Dr Timothy Leary and expounded by Robert Anton Wilson.

The Psychosynthesis model has been compared to its Kabbalistic counterpart in Jean Hardy's *A Psychology With A Soul*, and it is heartening to find that she states Kabbalah has a more effective model in this instance.[98] The circuit system has been matched to a Kabbalah scheme of YHVH and the tarot by Wilson in his unique workbook *Prometheus Rising*.

---

[98] Hardy, J. *A Psychology with a Soul*, p. 138.

Contemporary Kabbalah

In order to guide further studies from this present work, I have somewhat arbitrarily divided the contemporary field of Kabbalah into four categories; the scholarly; the new age; the esoteric and the literary. Whilst there are many overlaps between these categories, it may be a useful beginners guide that should you pursue one of these titles you will expect to be receiving a book full of dense historical information and heavily footnoted, a book focused on using the divine names to cleanse your Chakras, or a book of magical rituals and talismans, or a fictional piece weaving in many strands, all of which find their shelter under the spreading boughs and leafy arches of the Tree of Life.

The Scholarly

The most comprehensive overview of Kabbalah is provided by Gershom Scholem (1897 – 1982) in *Kabbalah* (1974) and other titles including *On Kabbalah and its Symbolism* (1965). Scholem brought to study of Kabbalah to prominence and also re-introduced it to the non-Jewish world from a historical perspective. The most contemporary writing on Kabbalah from a scholarly perspective is by Moshe Idel, in *Kabbalah: New Perspectives* (1990). Boaz Huss provides many references for contemporary approaches and studies across many viewpoints in his paper 'Contemporary Kabbalah and its Challenge to the Academic Study of Jewish Mysticism'.[99]

The work of Daniel C. Matt includes the latest translation of the *Zohar* (Pritzker Edition) and annotated extracts for study such as *The Essential Kabbalah* (2009) and *Zohar: Annotated and Explained* (2002).[100] Aryeh Kaplan (1934 – 1983) worked to explore science and Kabbalah and his later writings explored Jewish meditation techniques in *Meditation and Kabbalah* (1982). Authors such as

---

[99]

http://www.academia.edu/681812/Contemporary_Kabbalah_and_its_Challenge _to_the_Academic_Study_of_Jewish_Mysticism [Last accessed 13th June 2015]
[100] For the Pritzker Edition of the Zohar, see http://www.sup.org/zohar/ [Last accessed 13th June 2015].

Alexandre Safran have touched upon the relationship of Kabbalah to science, in *Wisdom of the Kabbalah* (1991).

The New Age

Esoteric authors, as we have seen, generally adopted Kabbalah through its earlier delivery by Levi, Mathers, Westcott, the Golden Dawn, Crowley and others. There was a later pickup of the system in a manner similar to the more widespread adoption of Yoga through what could generally be categorised (certainly by publishers) as "New Age" authors. These authors vary in their sources from 'traditional' Kabbalah to 'esoteric' Kabbalah.

A representative title in this category might be M. González-Wippler's *A Kabbalah for the Modern World* (1987) which features chapters on the Torah, Kabbalistic Magick and correspondences with other systems. Authors such as Will Parfitt in *Kabbalah for Life* (2006) introduce psychotherapy and counselling into the system, as well as providing exercises to contact extra-dimensional entities.

The Occult

The classic occult text on Kabbalah is surely Dion Fortune's *The Mystical Qabalah* (1935). Another influential book on western occultists is Gareth Knight's *A Practical Guide to Qabalistic Symbolism* in two volumes (1986). Israel Regardie's *Tree of Life* (1969) provides a wide-ranging summary of Kabbalah in the context of the Golden Dawn teachings and his work with Crowley.

Contemporary authors developing earlier esoteric work include Naomi Ozaniec, *The Aquarian Qabalah* (2003) whose work follows Dion Fortune through Dolores Ashcroft-Nowicki. An overview of the Tree of Life in terms of the initiatory ascent narrative can be discovered in Denning & Phillips, *Entrance to the Magical Qabalah* (1997). The work of Paul Foster Case and the B.O.T.A. organisation is more recently re-presented by Jason C. Lotterhand in *The Spoken Cabala* (2010).

The system as a whole is covered in detail in my own work, *The Magister* (2015). An accessible workbook from an O.T.O.

perspective (drawing on the work of Aleister Crowley) is given by Anita Kraft in *The Qabalah: Workbook for Magicians* (2013).

The Popular & Literary

Kabbalah has more recently been popularised by celebrity take-up through the Kabbalah Centre, most notably Madonna.[101] However, it has always been of attraction to those in the circles of imagination, creativity, arts, sciences and any endeavour of discovery. No less than British Poet Laureate Ted Hughes (1930 – 1998) wrote on Kabbalah, notably with regard to Shakespeare, suggesting that the practice of Kabbalah could help explain Shakespeare's "imaginative development, quite apart from his apparent attitude to religion and his handling of myths".[102]

The graphic novel *Promethea* by Alan Moore extensively draws upon Kabbalah.[103] There is a dense and complex use of Kabbalah in the work of Umberto Eco, particularly *Foucault's Pendulum* (1988), which is based on Lurianic Kabbalah and has sections named after each *Sephirah* down the Tree of Life. A similar use of Kabbalah can be found in the short stories of Jorge Luis Borges, such as *Labyrinths* (1962).

---

[101] See Myers, J. *Kabbalah and the Spiritual Quest: The Kabbalah Centre in America* (2007).
[102] Hughes, T. *Shakespeare and the Goddess of Complete Being*, p. 21.
[103] Moore, A. Art by J.H. Williams III & Mick Gray, *Promethea* (D.C. Comics).

Conclusion

In the opening of this book, we provided a brief quote from a previously unpublished note in the Golden Dawn archives, likely written by one of the three founders of the Order, S. L. MacGregor Mathers. The note was this:

> It was by the knowledge of the attribution of the Paths and the Tarot keys that Daniel deciphered the meaning of the MENE, MENE, TEKEL UPHARSIN.

This note and the mysterious words refer to the biblical story of Belshazzar's Feast, where a mysterious hand appeared and wrote upon the wall an undecipherable inscription.[104] It was the prophet Daniel who interpreted the writing, stating that it referred to not only the weights meant by the words, but drew from their sources; to be numbered, weighed and divided. In this, he interpreted that the King had been numbered by God, weighed and found wanting, and his Kingdom would fall and be divided. This came to pass that very night when the King was slain.

This idea - obviously embraced by the Golden Dawn - is a direct continuation of the first writing on the correspondence of the tarot to Hebrew letters with which we started this present book, as in Comte de Mellet's essay published in 1781, he stated (erroneously) that the biblical prophets used tarot to decipher dreams and visions. The Order of the Golden Dawn saw that through correspondence, all mysteries could be resolved, both of the past, present and future.

The note also teaches that we should learn correspondences in order to read the writing on the wall – for it is from this story we derive that popular phrase. When we "see the writing on the wall" it means that we are given insight into something that is in front of us, something that is already happening, and is unlikely to be

---

[104] Daniel. 5

avoided. However, by being able to use the Tree of Life and tarot to see that writing everywhere; the writing of the unfolding of existence, we can better prepare and align ourselves with that creation and in doing so, become truly one with the very word of the divine.

It is our hope that we have encouraged you a little more in this book to explore the mysteries of creation through Kabbalah and tarot, and we look forward to welcoming you in the Crucible if you decide to further enter the fire with us.[105]

---

[105] Join the Crucible Club at www.westernesotericism.com for studies and work in the WEIS.

Appendix: A Kabbalah Study Program

Whilst there are many ways of advancing your appreciation of Kabbalah and integration of its philosophy and practicality in your life, through both study and exercise, I would like to recommend here several avenues I have found most useful over the course of over thirty years work.

This is entirely contextualised in the Western Esoteric Initiatory System, so will not be the same as a study program in the context Jewish History or Religious Thought. However, you may find it a useful starting point for further studies alongside the material and exercises in this present book.

These are given as a few signposts and landmarks in a large landscape of study, and you are encouraged to go exploring as you will far beyond these marker points on the map and neither should you take these in any particular order in your own journey.

The exercises and reading lists in this present book are reasonably extensive and should be considered a more complete Travellers Guide to this brief list.

1. Acquire a Hebrew-English Dictionary. Whilst you do not need to learn fluent Hebrew to approach Kabbalah from this perspective, you should be aware of the power of the alphabet and the formation of words in Hebrew for even a basic appreciation of Kabbalah. I use Ben Yehuda's Pocket English-Hebrew/Hebrew-English Dictionary.

2. Get a general book on the Kabbalah to accompany your first steps, including *The Magician's Kabbalah* from an esoteric perspective [from which this list is taken] and the very accessible *The Kabbalah Decoder* by Janet Berens-Perkins.

3. For absolute beginners from the tarot world, we have written *Kabbalah and Tarot for Kindle* as 'Andrea Green'.

4. Learn the Hebrew alphabet, practice drawing the characters and learn their values.

5. Practice drawing the Tree of Life and learn the spellings and names of the *Sephiroth*.

6. Learn the correspondences of the tarot cards to the paths of the Tree of Life. Start with the Golden Dawn system, with a mind to Aleister Crowley's variation, and later switch to the Waite-Trinick model. This will allow you to first unlock most contemporary esoteric writing which uses the former system and then later develop further through the mind-set change that comes about with moving to a new system.

7. Study the nature of the *Sephiroth*, using Y. David Shulman's *The Sefirot*.

8. Study the nature of the Letters, using Edward Hoffman's *The Hebrew Alphabet* and Lawrence Kushner's *The Book of Letters*.

9. Build up your awareness of the *Sepher Yetzirah* as you build up your knowledge of the Letters.

10. Study the history of Kabbalah in *Major Trends in Jewish Mysticism* by Gershom G. Scholem and specific ideas in his *On the Kabbalah and its Symbolism*.

11. Go deeper with Aryeh Kaplan's *Kabbalah and Meditation* and *Kabbalah of Prayer* by Shulamit Elson.

12. Learn about the relationship of Christianity and Kabbalah starting with Ernst Benz's *Christian Kabbalah*.

13. Continue to make correspondences between the tarot, the Letters, and their positions on the Tree to your own experience. Begin to read works within Western Esotericism such as Dion Fortune's *Mystical Qabalah* to see how the Kabbalah was appropriated into the system.

14. As you progress, acquire the classic texts of Kabbalah, including the *Zohar* (annotated) or the full set of volumes such as the *Pritzker Edition*.

15. Further classic source works include the *Bahir, Gates of Light* and the *Tanya*.

16. Discover how Kabbalah can be mapped across to psychology in *Psychology with a Soul* by Jean Hardy and *Kabbalah and Psychology* by Z'ev ben Shimon Halevi.

17. As much of Western Esotericism derives from a Lurianic model of Kabbalah, to go back to the original source, see *Kabbalah of Creation: Isaac Luria's Earlier Mysticism*, translated by Eliahu Klein.

Bibliography

Albertson, E. *Understanding the Kabbalah*. Sherbourne Press: Los Angeles, 1973.

Ashe, E. (ed). *The Hermetic Kabbalah of Anna Kingsford*. Glastonbury Books: Glastonbury, 2006.

Auger, E. (ed). *Tarot in Culture Vol I*. Valleyhome Books, 2014.

Bain, D., Goodwin, T. & Katz, M. *A New Dawn for Tarot: The Original Tarot of the Golden Dawn*. Forge Press: Keswick, 2014.

Bain, D., Goodwin, T., Katz, M. & Hall, J. *The Tarot of the Secret Dawn* (Deck & Book). Forge Press: Keswick, 2015.

Bardon, F. *The Key to the True Quabbalah*. Dieter Rüggeberg: Wuppertal, 1975.

Beitchman, P. *Alchemy of the Word*. State University of New York Press: Albany, 1998.

Benz, C. *Christian Kabbalah*. Grailstone Press: St. Paul, 2004.

Bentov, I. *Stalking the Wild Pendulum*. Destiny Books: Rochester, 1988.

Bonder, N. *The Kabbalah of Envy*. Shambala: Boston & London, 1997.

Borges, J. L. *Labyrinths*. Penguin: London, 1970.

Christopher, L. T. *Kabbalah Magic*. Llewellyn: Woodbury, 2006.

Cohen, M. & Cohen, Y. (ed). *In the Shadow of the Ladder*. Nehora Press: Safed, 2002.

Cooper, D. A. *God is a Verb*. Riverhead Books: New York, 1998.

Crowley, A. *Magical and Philosophical Commentaries on the Book of the Law*. 93 Publishing: Montréal, 1974.

Crowley, A. *Magick*. Guild Publishing: 1989.

---- *Konx om Pax*. Yogi Publication Society, n.d.

Dan, J. *The Early Kabbalah*. Paulist Press: New York, 1986.

Davis, A. *The Way of the Flame*. Jewish Lights Publishing: Woodstock, 1999.

Denning, M. & Phillips, O. *Entrance to the Magical Qabalah*. Thoth Publications: Loughborough, 1997.

Drob, S. L. *Symbols of the Kabbalah*. Jason Aronson: Northvale, 2000.

Eco, U. *Foucault's Pendulum*. Vintage: London, 2001.

Elson, S. *Kabbalah of Prayer*. Lindisfarme Books: Great Barrington, 2004.

Farr, F. *Egyptian Magic*. Aquarian Press: Wellingborough, 1982.

Fine, L. *Physician of the Soul, Healer of the Cosmos*. Stanford University Press: Stanford, 2003.

Fishbane, E. P. *As Light Before the Dawn*. Stanford University Press: Stanford, 2009.

Fortune, D. *The Mystical Qabalah*. Ernest Benn Ltd: London & Tonbridge, 1979.

Ginsberg, C. D. *The Essenes, The Kabbalah (Two Essays)*. Routledge & Kegan Paul: London, 1956.

Gleick, J. *Chaos*. Sphere Books: London, 1988.

Goddard, D. *The Tree of Sapphires*. Samuel Weiser: York Beach, 2004.

González-Wippler, M. *A Kabbalah for the Modern World*. Llewellyn, St. Paul: 1987.

Goodwin, T. & Katz, M. *Abiding in the Sanctuary: The Waite-Trinick Tarot (1917-1923)*. Forge Press: Keswick, 2011.

    ---- *Secrets of the Waite-Smith Tarot*. Llewellyn: St. Paul, 2015.

Grant, K. *Outside the Circles of Time*. Frederick Muller: London, 1980.

Gray, W. G. *Growing the Tree Within*. Llewellyn: St. Paul, 1991.

Gray, W. G. *Qabalistic Concepts*. Samuel Weiser: York Beach, 1997.

Green, A. *Kabbalah and Tarot*. Forge Press: Keswick, 2015.

Halevi, Z. b. S. *A Kabbalistic Universe*. Gateway Books: Bath, 1977.

    ---- *Kabbalah and Psychology*. Gateway Books: Bath, 1986.

    ---- *School of the Soul*. Gateway Books: Bath, 1985. (prev. *School of Kabbalah*)

    ---- *The Way of Kabbalah*. Rider: London, n.d.

Hallamish, M. *An Introduction to Kabbalah*. State University Press of New York: Albany, 1999.

Hanson, G. *Dynamic Kabbalah*. Xlibris: 2003.

Hanson, K. *Kabbalah*. Council Oak Books: Tulsa and San Francisco, 1998.

Hellner-Eshed, M. *A River Flows From Eden*. Stanford University Press: Stanford, 2009.

Hoffman, E. (ed). *Opening the Inner Gates*. Shamballa: Boston & London, 1995.

---- *The Heavenly Ladder*. Prism Press: Sturminster Newton, 1996.

---- *The Hebrew Alphabet*. Chronicle Books: San Francisco, 1998.

Hopking, C. J. M. *The Practical Kabbalah Guidebook*. Godsfield Press: Newton Abbot, 2001.

Hughes, T. *Shakespeare and the Goddess of Complete Being*. Faber & Faber: London, 1992.

Hundert, G. D. (ed.) *Essential Papers on Hasidism*. New York University Press: New York, 1991.

Idel, M. *Absorbing Perfections*. Yale University Press: New Haven & London, 2002.

---- *Ascensions on High in Jewish Mysticism*. Central European University Press: Budapest, 2005.

---- *Kabbalah: New Perspectives*. Yale University Press: New Haven, 1988.

---- *Studies in Ecstatic Kabbalah*. State University of New York Press: Albany, 1988.

---- *The Mystical Experience in Abraham Abulafia*. State University of New York Press: Albany, 1988.

Kaplan, A. (trans.) *The Bahir*. Samuel Weiser: York Beach, 1979.

---- *Inner Space*. Moznaim Publishing: New York, 1990.

---- *Jewish Meditation*. Schocken Books: New York, 1985.

---- *Meditation and Kabbalah*. Samuel Weiser: York Beach, 1982.

---- *The Lost Princess & Other Kabbalistic Tales of Rebbe Nachman of Breslov*. Jewish Lights Publishing: Woodstock, 2005.

Karlson, T. *Qabalah, Qliphoth and Goetic Magic*. Ajna: Jacksonville, 2012.

Katz, M. *The Magister (Vol 0)*. Salamander & Sons: Chiang Mai, 2015.

---- *Tarosophy*. Salamander & Sons: Chiang Mai, 2011.

Kempis, T. *The Imitation of Christ*. Dover Books: Mineola, 2003.

Klein, E. (trans). *Kabbalah of Creation: Issac Luria's Earlier Mysticism*. Jason Aronson: Northvale, 2000.

Knight, G. *A Practical Guide to Qabalistic Symbolism* (2 vols). Kahn & Averil: London, 1986.

Kraft, A. *The Qabalah: Workbook for Magicians*. Weiser: San Francisco, 2013.

Krakovsky, L. I. *Kabbalah: The Light of Redemption*. Research Centre of Kabbalah: Jerusalem, 1970.

Kramer, C. *Hidden Treasures*. Breslov Research Institute: Jerusalem, 2007.

Kramer, S. Z. *Hidden Faces of the Soul*. Adams Media Corporation: Holbrook, 2000.

Küntz, D. (ed.) *The Complete Golden Dawn Cipher Manuscript*. Holmes Publishing Group: Edmonds, 1996.

Kushner, L. *Honey from the Rock*. Jewish Lights Publishing: Woodstock, 1994.

---- *The Book of Letters*. Jewish Lights Publishing: Woodstock, 1990.

---- *The Book of Words*. Jewish Lights Publishing: Woodstock, 1998.

Lampert, V. *Practical Kabbalah for Magic and Protection*. Cico Books: London, 2002.

Laos, N. *The Kairological Qabalah*. White Crane Publishing: Northampton, 2012.

Levi, E. *The Book of Splendours*. Aquarian Press: Wellingborough, 1983.

---- *The History of Magic*. Rider & Company: London, 1982.

---- *The Key of the Mysteries*. Rider & Company: London, 1984.

---- *The Magical Ritual of the Sanctum Regnum*. Ibis Press: Berwick, 2004.

---- *Transcendental Magic*. Bracken Books: London, 1995.

Libet, B. *Mind Time*. Harvard University Press: Cambridge, 2005.

Lotterhand, J. C. *The Spoken Cabala*. Fraternity of Hidden Light Publications, 2010.

Maimonides. *The Guide of the Perplexed*. Hackett Publishing Company: Indianapolis & Cambridge, 1995.

Mathers, S. L. M. *The Kabbalah Unveiled*. Routledge & Kegan Paul: London, 1981.

---- *The Tarot*. Unicorn Bookshop: Brighton, Seattle, n.d.

Matt, D. C. *The Essential Kabbalah*. HarperCollins: New York, 1994.

---- *Zohar: Annotated & Explained*. Skylight Paths: Woodstock, 2002.

Menzi, D. W. & Padeh, Z. *The Tree of Life: Chayyim Vital's Introduction to the Kabbalah of Isaac Luria*. Arizal Publications: New York, 2008.

Moslowitz, L. (trans). *The Soul of Life: The Complete Neffesh Ha-Chayyim*. New Davar Publications: Teaneck, 2012.

Myers, J. *Kabbalah and the Spiritual Quest: The Kabbalah Centre in America*. Prager: Santa Barbara, 2007.

Nichols, S. *Jung and Tarot*. Samuel Weiser: York Beach, 1984.

Papus. *The Qabalah*. Thorsons: Wellingborough, 1977.

Parfitt, W. *Kabbalah for Life*. Rider: London, 2006.

Perkins, K. & Johnson, K. *Egyptian Life and the Tree of Life*. International Order of Kabbalists, 1982.

Plato, (ed. Warrington, J.) *Timaeus*. Dent: London, 1965.

Regardie, I. *The Golden Dawn* (6th edition). Llewellyn: St. Paul, 1989.

---- *The Tree of Life*. Aquarian Press, Wellingborough, 1980.

Reuchlin, J. (trans. Goodman, M. & Goodman, S.) *On the Art of the Kabbalah*. University of Nebraska Press: Lincoln and London, 1993.

Ribner, M. *Everyday Kabbalah*. Citadel Press: Secaucus, 1998.

Roland, P. *The Complete Kabbalah Course*. Quantum: London, 2005.

Rojtman, B. *Black Fire on White Fire*. University of California Press: Berkeley & Los Angeles, 1998.

Safran, A. *Wisdom of the Kabbalah*. Feldheim Publishers: Jerusalem, 1991.

Scholem, G. *Kabbalah*. Dorset Press: New York, 1974.

---- *Major Trends in Jewish Mysticism*. Schocken Books: New York, 1961.

---- *Origins of the Kabbalah*. Princeton University Press: Princeton, 1990.

Shapiro, R. M. *Minyan*. Bell Tower: New York, 1997.

Sheinkin, D. *Path of the Kabbalah*. Paragon House: New York, 1986.

Shulman, Y.D. *The Sefirot*. Jason Aronson: Northvale, 1996.

Sperling, H. & Simon, M. (trans). *The Zohar* [5 vol]. The Soncino Press: London, 1984.

Steinsaltz, A. *Opening the Tanya*. Jossey-Bass: San Francisco, 2003.

---- *The Thirteen Petalled Rose*. Basic Books: New York, 1980.

Stewart, R. J. *The Miracle Tree*. New Page Books: Franklin Lakes, 2003.

Strassfield, M. *A Book of Life*. Schocken Books: New York, 2002.

Sturzaker, D. & Sturzaker, J. *Colour and the Kabbalah*. Thorsons: Wellingborough, 1975.

Suarès, C. *The Qabala Trilogy*. Shambhala Publications: Boston, 1976.

---- *The Song of Songs*. Shambhala Publications, Berkley, 1972.

Turner, D. *The Darkness of God*. Cambridge University Press: Cambridge, 1995.

Waite, A. E. *Steps to the Crown*. Philip Welby: London, 1907.

Weiner, H. *9 ½ Mystics: The Kabbalah Today*. Macmillan: New York, 1991.

Weinstein, A. (trans). *Gates of Light*. Harper Collins: San Francisco, 1994.

Westcott, W. W. *An Introduction to the Study of the Kabbalah*. Metaphysical Research Group: Hastings, 1978.

Wilson, R. A. Prometheus Rising. Falcon Press: Phoenix, 1986.

Winkler, G. *Magic of the Ordinary: Recovering the Shamanic in Judaism*. North Atlantic Books: Berkeley, 2003.

Kindle Tarot Books & Series

Check out all our other books and series for original and exciting ways in which you can use a deck of tarot cards to change your life.

Gated Spreads Series

Set 1

Book 1: The Tarot Shaman (Contact Your Animal Spirit)

Book 2: Gates of Valentine (Love & Relationships)

Book 3: The Resurrection Engine (Change Your Life)

Set 2

Book 4: Palace of the Phoenix (Alchemy)

Book 5: Garden of Creation (Creativity & Inspiration)

Book 6: Ghost Train (Explore Your Past)

Set 3

Tarot Temple

Book 1: Create a Tarot Dream Temple

Book 2: The Sacred Altar

Book 3: Tarot Temple Tools

Book 4: Banishing Negativity & Unbalanced Forces

Book 5: Purification of your Temple & Life

Book 6: Consecration of your Temple & Life

Book 7: Divining with the Gods

Tarosophy KickStart Series

Volume I.

Book I: Tarot Flip - Reading Tarot Straight from the Box

Book II: Tarot Twist – 78 New Spreads and Methods [paperback]

Book III: Tarot Inspire – Tarot for a Spiritual Life

Tarot Life Series

Tarot Life: A revolutionary method to change your life in 12 Kindle booklets. Also includes membership of a private discussion group on Facebook to share and explore your experiences with over a thousand other readers.

1. Discover Your Destiny

2. Remove The Blocks

3. Make Decisions Better

4. Enter the Flow

5. Ride the Lion

6. Connect to Service

7. Find Equality

8. Die To Your Self

9. Entering Unity

10. Becoming the Real

11. Your Keys to Freedom

12. The Depth of Divinity

Also in Print and Kindle

Tarosophy: A ground-breaking book packed with original ideas. The book also includes 50 unique exercises for Tarot and an extended method of using the Inner Guide Meditation as given here.

Around the Tarot in 78 Days: The ideal beginner book, a three-month course through every card. An award-winning book, recognized by the COVR New Age Industry Award for Best Divination Book 2013.

Tarot Face to Face: Take your tarot out of the box and into life!

The Secrets of the Waite-Smith Tarot: Learn the real meanings of the world's most popular tarot deck [Spring 2015, pub. Llewellyn Worldwide].

Tarot Turn Vol. 1 - 3: A massive crowd-sourced reference guide to all 12,200 possible combinations of reversed Tarot card pairs.

Websites & Resources

If you enjoy new learning, and want many more ways to use your Tarot deck, we encourage you to explore our websites. You are also welcome to join us in your national Tarosophy Tarot Association, where as a member you will instantly receive thousands of pages of materials, and tarot video courses for every level.

We look forward to seeing you soon on your Tarot journey!

Tarosophy Tarot Associations

http://www.tarotassociation.net

Tarot Professionals Facebook Group

http://www.facebook.com/groups/tarotprofessionals

Free Tarot Card Meanings & Spreads

http://www.mytarotcardmeanings.com

Hekademia Tarot Course

http://www.tarosophyuniversity.com

Tarot Town Social Network

http://www.tarot-town.com

Tarosophy by Marcus Katz

http://www.tarosophy.com

The Tarot Speakeasy Blog

http://www.tarotspeakeasy.com

Tarot Book Club

http://www.tarotbookclub.com

The Tarot Review

http://www.thetarotreview.com

TarotCon International Tarot Conventions

http://www.tarotconvention.com

Fortune-Telling Laws

http://www.fortunetellinglaws.com

The Original Lenormand Deck

http://www.originallenormand.com

Learning Lenormand

http://www.learninglenormand.com

www.ingramcontent.com/pod-product-compliance
Lightning Source LLC
LaVergne TN
LVHW051501080426
835509LV00017B/1855